6-13-74

OFFICE SPACE ADMINISTRATION

Kenneth H. Ripnen, R. A., N.C.A.R.B., A.I.A.

Chief Executive Architect, The Ripnen Company
Office Space Administration Consultants
Division of Ripnen Architects, P.C.
New York City

Member: American Management Association, Inc.,
Administrative Management Society (formerly N.O.M.A.)
Committee Member, Office Environment Research Committee;
The Real Estate Board of New York, Inc.; New York
Building Congress; The Architectural League of New York;
National Institute for Architectural Education (formerly
Beaux-Arts Institute of Design); National Sculpture Society
(Honorary Member)

McGRAW-HILL BOOK COMPANY

New York   St. Louis   San Francisco   Düsseldorf
Johannesburg   Kuala Lumpur   London   Mexico
Montreal   New Delhi   Panama   Paris
São Paulo   Singapore   Sydney
Tokyo   Toronto

Library of Congress Cataloging in Publication Data

Ripnen, Kenneth H
  Office space administration.

Published in 1960 under title: Office building
and office layout planning.
  1. Office layout.   I. Title.
HF5547.R55   1974   651'.32   73-9801
ISBN 0-07-052936-1

1234567890 VHVH 7654

The editors for this book were W. Hodson Mogan, Gretlyn Blau,
and Robert E. Curtis, the designer was Naomi Auerbach, and
its production was supervised by Teresa F. Leaden. It was
set in Optima Medium by Progressive Typographers.

It was printed and bound by Von Hoffman Press, Inc.

To my patient and loving wife

and

to those executives and their staff assistants
who are responsible for office space standards,
space assignment, and furniture and layout planning
so that office workers may be properly housed
and equipped to carry out their responsibilities
comfortably and efficiently — and to architects, engineers,
manufacturers of building materials and furniture,
and others interested and involved in office architecture,
in order that they may gain new insights
into the problems facing those they serve.

1802818

CONTENTS

FOREWORD

Economic and wise planning and proper selection of neighborhood and building is most essential to the business success of any tenant, large or small. Proper location for the tenant is the first essential. Next comes the proper building that will speed up and give the tenant every advantage of science that this atomic and electronic age has provided. Area of floors must be studied for the various types of tenants' occupancy so as to speed up its business: sequence of departments is most necessary. Guidance by the best of specialists in office planning and construction of individual building is a prime necessity.

Today, with office building construction at its peak, supplying office space to satisfy our continuous growing economy, along with new developments in business efficiency, architecture and engineering, a summation and forecast of the best in many related techniques for solving office building and office space planning, construction, equipping, and maintenance problems is needed.

I can think of no person more qualified than Kenneth H. Ripnen to present ways and means to those interested in office space to assist them in solving their problems.

Mr. Ripnen, schooled as an architect, served his apprenticeship in architects' offices, and after 12 years of intensive experience, received a most important appointment, that of office space architect for the War Department in World War II, expediting the Army Headquarters organization's occupancy of The Pentagon and the later administering of the War Department's office buildings, which housed 60,000 office workers, both military and civilian. Therefore it is little wonder that his services have been in demand from our leading business interests.

From personal knowledge of his career and through business relations over the years of his business life, I have known his work and his success.

I have discussed with Mr. Ripnen most intimate details of office building and construction as related to efficient and economical office planning; I can say that his book and presentations should be invaluable to anyone concerned with the subject of office space and should be in the office of any large owner of real estate and every real estate manager of important buildings.

Charles F. Noyes

INTRODUCTION

The aim of all that is written here is to aid in the planning of the best possible office layout—one that provides complete flexibility, is efficient and economical, satisfies all functional arrangements, is comfortable for the worker, creates an impression of spaciousness in the most crowded areas and permits a system of office space control. Ideally, an office architect determines the present and future requirements of the office in terms of space, personnel, equipment, and furniture, and the flow of work and interrelationships between workers and departments; then, drawing on his knowledge of the design, mechanical and structural aspects of architecture and on his knowledge of materials, furniture, and facilities that exist, he plans and designs the best possible layout and building.

Of course, not every company has the need for a new office building; but every company does have a need for space of some kind, and its needs frequently change. It is the aim of this book to aid those responsible for planning for changing office space needs.

Specifically, the functions of the office space planner, or space administrator, are examined and his relationship to management described, office space standards are discussed, techniques for determining space needs are presented in detail, and there is a thorough discussion of layout planning. Since a large number of companies seeking additional office space find it in older structures, there is a chapter on building modernization; a chapter on planning the move to new space has also been included.

The following portion of the text is aimed primarily at those companies contemplating the construction of a new office building. Such considerations as types of buildings, site location, selection of the architect, and planning the building are discussed, followed by an examination of the importance of working drawings, specifications, estimates, contracts, and schedules.

Finally, a look at the office of the future is offered.

The planning of office space has passed through several stages since World War II, and a brief look at them will be of value to anyone charged with responsibilities in this area. (See Illustration A-1.) In the first stage—let us call it Phase I—the architect was generally responsible for the structure, spatial conditioning, furniture, and layout planning standards. Architects designed the buildings, and with the client, planned and designed the offices. Frequently there was a general office work area with files and low divider walls separating workers, sections, and supervisors. Conventional ceiling-high partitions were used to enclose executive offices, departments, and corridors.

However, in the larger urban areas the architect for the structure was rarely able to maintain influence over the design and planning problems of tenants of commercial space rentals. Hence a new group of space planners, sometimes dubbed "space cadets," appeared on the horizon, offering to plan and equip offices for tenants of commercial skyscrapers. The result was a design trend toward office space layout and furniture design that had no relationship to building structure because lighting, air conditioning, egress, and ceiling-high partitions integrated with the structure were all the architect's responsibility, not the space planner's. We can identify this as Phase II, the open office period, starting a little before 1960. There was a departure from the conventional layout featuring corridors, partitioned private offices, and adjacent open areas with aligned rows of desks. The open office approach featured "freely" arranged furniture or work stations, placed to coincide with work flow and communication

Illus. A-1. Stages in office planning. (*The Ripnen Company, The Eggers Partnership.*)

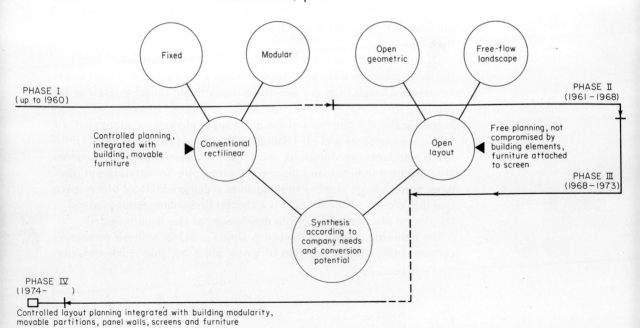

networks of the office departments and office workers. The private areas were separated by free-standing low dividers and planters, assembled without influence of basic office traffic lanes or straight corridors. (See Illustration A-2.) Executives and supervisors were put in the new bull pen, socializing our concepts of office planning.

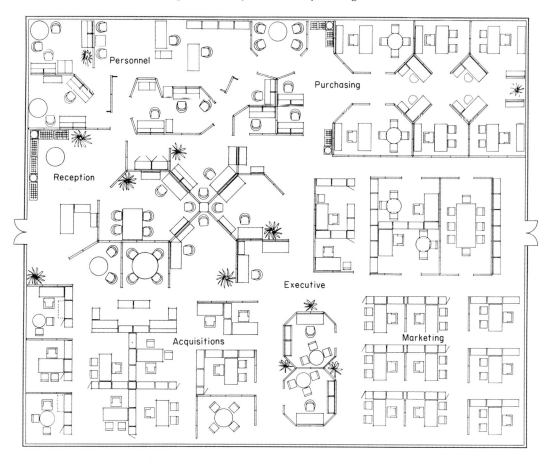

Illus. A-2. Open office. (Above) Layout. (Right) Low partition. (Steelcase Inc.)

Phase III developed as an extension of the ideas of free and open planning of Phase II. The low screen or dividing partition soon became the place to hang work surfaces, supplanting the conventional office desk. It also provided for the hanging of lateral files, cupboards, tack boards, and accessories. No furniture touched the floor. The all-supporting low screen also provided telephone and electric outlets. (See Illustrations A-3 and A-4.) Like Phase II design, this concept was carried out without reference to or coordination with structure, except for necessary access to building services.

Illus. A-3. Open office — screen and components. (Steelcase Inc.)

Illus. A-4. Open office — screen and lateral file. (Royal Metal.)

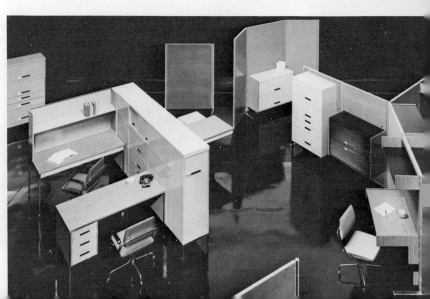

Meanwhile, since 1960, architects, engineers, manufacturers of building material, and some manufacturers of office furniture and partitions continued the process of research and development with the goal of successful total controlled modularity. As used in this book, "total modularity" refers to the total integration of office work-station furniture, facilities, partitions, spatial conditioning, and structure in order to permit complete flexibility in the planning of office layout arrangements. Office furniture manufacturers' design theme continued with the belief that desks and related furnishings are movable, salvageable items of a better than conventional design. In Phase IV, as we shall call it, high-profile or two-legged, two-drawer pedestal desks, with adjacent credenzas or lateral files and cabinets, satisfied most workers' requirements. All were designed to minimize bulk and create an illusion of spaciousness. (See Illustrations A-5 and A-6.) Where isolation was necessary for privacy or for other reasons, a floor-to-ceiling panelwall could be installed with relative ease in an appropriately grooved modular ceiling and integrated with lighting and air conditioning. (See Illustration A-7.) The panelwall could have an acoustical surface treatment or other finishes and could be equiped with telephone and electric outlets. The subject of total modularity will be gone into in considerable detail in the text, as we are convinced of its preeminent position in the field of office space planning. The building best exemplifying total modularity is that of the U.S. Steel Corporation in Pittsburgh, shown in Illustrations A-8a and A-8b.

Illus. A-5. Open desk design. (Cramer Industires.)

Illus. A-6. Open furniture accessories design. (Cramer Industries.)

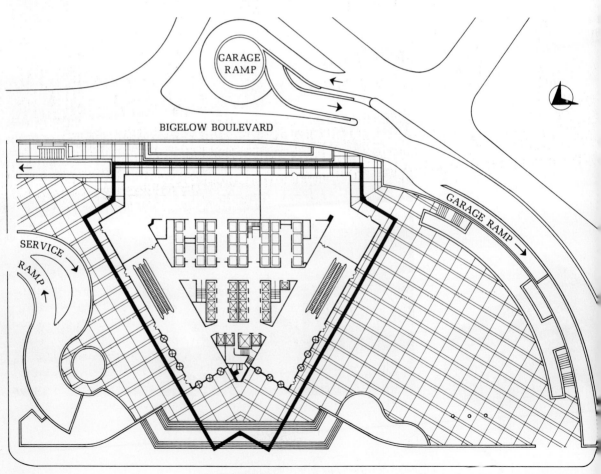

GARAGE RAMP

BIGELOW BOULEVARD

GARAGE RAMP

SERVICE RAMP

GRANT STREET

Illus. A-7. (Left) Panelwall design. (E. F. Hauserman Co.)

Illus. A-8. U.S. Steel building. (Left) ~~Si~~te plan. (Right) Elevation. (U.S. ~~St~~eel Corp.)

The planning of office space requires the cooperation of many talents. Today, contracts for construction of urban and suburban office buildings to be occupied by tenant-owners require that the architectural firm for the project have a team of architectural, engineering, and office layout planning people, and work closely with the owner's team, in order to accomplish the best in office layout planning totally integrated with the architectural and engineering elements of the office building. The importance of management consultant engineering assistance on the team cannot be overstressed. Such management experts can take the responsibility of confirming and documenting the client's staffing, systems, work flow, relationship of departments and individuals, and future expansion plans.

Mr. R. C. Walters, Executive Director of the Administrative Management Society, has said "It has been stated that a 'Third Corporate Profit' is realized by companies when their office building and office facilities for office space are up to standard—this profit follows those made through, first, increased sales and, second, more efficient production." Let us now take a look at how office space planning, the responsibility of the office space administrator, proceeds.

one

THE OFFICE SPACE
ADMINISTRATOR

AREAS OF RESPONSIBILITY

Throughout this book we shall be referring to a person called the "space administrator"—the individual in the company who determines the number of square feet for departmental space allotment, who has primary responsibility for the planning and layout of office quarters and for ensuring that departments, office workers, machines, and records are placed in the most logical space relationship to each other. It is also his job to ensure that all needed facilities are included in the office layout and that the layout in general is the most functional space arrangement possible in terms of the company's needs and purposes.

But as we shall see, an office layout plan is not a static thing, permanent once it has been established. As the company's needs change, as the work of departments varies, space rearrangements will be necessary within the existing office. Therefore, the layout must be made flexible through proper planning of physical, mechanical, and structural facilities. Continued office space administration and maintenance, in other words, is just as important a job as the original space planning.

Who should be responsible for controlling space in the office, once that office has been established and is a working entity?

Management's prime concern is the over-all guidance of the company; it should always be free to concern itself with the company's products,

9

markets, distribution problems. It employs adminstrators to plan the details by which its objectives and major policies may be achieved; it should not itself be concerned with these details. And proper coordination of space for the most efficient work pattern is an administrative or specialized function rather than a management function.

By the same token, the office manager has as his primary responsibility the smooth functioning of office services. He is an administrator who must coordinate personnel, machines, work-flow scheduling, and a host of other details so that the work of the company goes through as smoothly, quickly, and economically as possible.

As a matter of economy in the very small company, it may be necessary to assign the entire space-administration function to the office manager in addition to his other duties. But in larger concerns, space administration is enough of a responsibility to require a full-time administrator and, in some instances, a staff.

In cases where such an administrator is justified, it is his responsibility to keep in touch with the company's changing operations, personnel strength, methods and systems, and control and coordinate the company's office space in accordance with these changing needs. This means he must work closely with the office manager and department heads to keep in touch with their current and future requirements. He must also keep informed of new materials and equipment; he must have an over-all plan or concept for control of the space available; and he must ensure that his solutions to day-by-day space problems are in accordance with the over-all plan.

Yet it is his responsibility, too, to handle the day-by-day changes in space requests and requirements, to know which requests are justified and should be met, which should be partially met, which should be refused. If new space is needed for one department, the administrator must know where to find it. And he must frame all these changing requirements in terms of the basic elements of the over-all layout plan, so that changes in the amount of space given various departments do not compromise the plan — or himself. This is why it is so important that standards be established in the first place. They serve as a measuring stick by which the justification of requests can be evaluated.

These responsibilities of space administration emphasize again why the integrated space layout and standardization of equipment and furniture throughout the organization are so important in terms of meeting changing space requirements with a minimum of time, trouble, and interference with the work flow of the office. It is the fact that frequent changes are necessary that makes movable partitions, furniture in standard sizes and colors, modular construction of physical and mechanical elements so important in the planning phases of office layout. All these factors are insurance that the office space will be adaptable when the time comes for changes in interior layout arrangements.

The tools of the space administrator are his records and current informational data on the organization, its procedures, and personnel. His records are master sets of up-to-date reference drawings and office layouts of the space he is responsible for. These would include:

1. A blank plan of the premises, showing fixed elements of the office building and its available office space with dotted lines to indicate the basic circulation plan leading to all services and usable space for allotment identified by bay or room numbers with the area for each unit of space.

2. A copy of this plan should be colored to show what areas are assigned to major departments of the company, so that ready reference can be made to these areas and the total number of square feet assigned to each department. This is the space-control plan.

3. An up-to-date office layout showing all partitions and department furniture and equipment in detail within each colored area.

4. An architectural and structural set of drawings, showing physical conditions of the premises and types of partitions.

5. A set of mechanical drawings containing overhead lighting, switch control, electric and telephone outlets, underfloor ducts, plumbing, heating, and air-conditioning information.

These drawings should be kept up to date at all times, and the space administrator should keep himself currently informed on all factors affecting organization, procedures, and personnel, so that he can anticipate changes and know where space will be needed or will become available through increases and decreases in personnel. He must keep abreast of this information if effective space control is to be exercised.

Preplanning, as well as maintenance of standards once the office has been established, is the space administrator's responsibility. What is his place in the organization structure?

It depends very much on the organization. Space administration in the office is a relatively new field. Different companies have placed space administration in different departments. There are good reasons for each of these assignments, and space administration has functioned well in each of them. Here is how some companies handle the space-administration function:

Space administrators may function directly under the vice-president in charge of central administrative services. In this position, the space administrator serves directly in the department which is responsible for most of the service and housekeeping functions of the organization and which also is in the best position to evaluate the validity of various departmental requests for extra space.

Alternatively, the space administrator may function under the head of the corporation's engineering department. This is logical in terms of the fact that space-administration duties include some designing, engineering, and construction. Also, in this organizational placement, the administrator will have easy access to the drafting and engineering services of the engineering department.

If the corporation has a real estate department, it often makes sense to place the space-administration group under its jurisdiction. This is particularly true of a corporation which is expanding rapidly and so is constantly planning new facilities. Obviously, in such a case, the company's real estate interests would be directly related to space-planning activities, and so it would be most logical to have all space-planning and maintenance functions part of the real estate department.

In other companies, it has been found advisable to have the space administrator work in conjunction with the systems or methods and procedures department. Depending on the size of the corporation, the space administrator may also work directly under the controller or treasurer, or under the executive vice-president as an independent entity.

In other words, many different places in the organization structure may be logical spots for the space administrator and his staff. The departments mentioned above all have functions with which space administration is concerned. The spot in any given company will depend on how that company is organized and whether administration of current space or planning of new space is the administrator's main function. The vital thing, no matter in which department the space-planning function is located, is that there be sufficient authority behind the space planner to allow him to do his job and to make his objective decisions about space assignment or reassignment without fear of having those decisions reversed. For the space planner's role is an important one and, if carried out by a qualified man with enough backing to make his decisions authoritative, can contribute as much to the company as such other major service departments as personnel, systems and procedures, and research. The essential thing is that the administrator be on the central-management team—the basic office-services group—which keeps the company operating smoothly.

No matter what department in the company the space administrator is assigned to, however, one fact should always be borne in mind by management: his role embraces a variety of responsibilities. He cannot operate in a vacuum. He will need outside services or, rather, services of other specialists from time to time, whether these specialists are drawn from within the company or from outside sources.

First of all, he needs information about the company and a continuing stream of information about the changing daily needs which it is his responsibility to meet, as well as forecasts and plans for future changes, such as mergers or relocation. This means he must have a general working knowledge of each department and its requirements. To give him this knowledge it is advisable to set up a "space committee" of company personnel with whom the administrator can work. Such a committee should include a representative for each department or division in the corporation and should function as a consulting group to the space administrator, aiding him particularly in evaluating departmental needs and in interpreting for him the procedures and methods by which the company office accomplishes its work. This is particularly important when the company has no methods and procedures department as such.

In addition to administering the space occupied by the company's offices, it is the duty of the space administrator to keep management informed concerning the office quarters, changes in departmental space requirements, and moves that have been made to meet anticipated new space requirements. In a word, he must keep management informed of current problems and their solutions and alerted to possible future problems with their possible alternative solutions. In addition, it is his duty to inform management of significant advances in office design and furnishings.

This is often done through a committee arrangement which helps the space planner foresee possible space problems that may arise in the future and also helps him arrive at the best possible solutions to those problems.

In presenting recommendations to management, which, after all, does not ordinarily involve itself in day-to-day operating problems, the space administrator should present the whole scope of the anticipated problem along with the recommended courses of action. The report to management should cover the following:

1. Statement of the problem

2. The tabulation or listing of facts about the problem in the form of plans showing required areas in terms of square feet, graphs, photographs, etc.

3. Conclusions drawn from the facts relating to the problem

4. Recommendations to management for possible solutions to the problem

Although there may be several alternative solutions to any given problem, the space administrator should not abdicate responsibility and simply present solutions without indicating which solution he thinks would be best. He has been placed in his present position as an administrator, as someone who should have opinions and reasons to back them up. He is certainly more than a maintenance man and can show a creative interest in his company and his work. Management may overrule his opinions, but it should be given the benefit of his advice as he is well founded on company operations.

This in turn implies that the space administrator must really be a specialist, that he must know not only the problems of the company but the techniques, terminology, and tools of the trade of architect or engineer.

The advances made in services and techniques for office building and office layout planning, furniture, and facilities today require constant research if one is to keep abreast of what is going on and what can be anticipated. It is only through the constant study of such current information that the optimum in efficiency of the office organization, as far as space administration is concerned, can be realized. The space administrator responsible for the maintenance of standards uses this material when submitting reports to bulwark and support his recommendations to management.

It may be necessary for the space administrator to call in outside consultants from time to time. This should not be taken as a sign of inadequacy on his part but rather as a symbol of maturity and knowledge of his job. Space planning and administration will require specialized advice from different fields, all of which cannot be mastered by any one person. The company that appoints a space administrator who recognizes that he can't be an expert on everything is much better off than the concern that has a man who attempts fields in which his knowledge is inadequate — and fails in the process, at company expense.

Among the typical outside specialists that the space administrator may have to call on for help from time to time are architects, engineers, landscape architects, real estate brokers, interior decorators, color consultants, engineering departments of manufacturers of specialized equipment, such as electronic units and conveyer systems.

Obviously, when a major project, such as construction of a building or extensive alteration or modernization of existing space, is planned, the intelligent space-administration department will call on the services of an architect. Choice of the architect may be made by the space administrator, by a company committee, or by management. In any event, it is essential that management approve the final choice of the outside architect.

No matter who makes the selection, it is important that the architect chosen be one of those approved or recommended by the space administrator, for the very simple reason that the latter will have to act as company liaison with that firm during the entire period of survey, planning, construction, or alteration. Moreover, he will also have to administer the new space after the architect has left and the company planning committees have been disbanded. And he is, by the very nature of his role and his job, better able than most company personnel to evaluate the qualifications of an architect for the particular job that must be done.

In conclusion, office space administration is no "extra duty" to be foisted off on someone who already has a full-time job — at least it is not in a large corporation. It is an important responsibility and a costly investment where the annual operation expense can be a large figure. If performed badly, it can have a tremendous effect on the working environment, the physical comfort of employees, company costs, and the efficiency with which the company carries out its daily operations. Physical factors have a definite effect on employee work output, just as good personnel policies do. They also have a distinct effect on the speed and accuracy with which work is accomplished, just as good systems planning does — there is no room for complacency in office space administration.

It is the role of the space administrator to see that the company's physical space and facilities promote efficiency and high morale just as it is the role of the systems planner to ensure that the company does its work in the best possible manner and of the personnel director to ensure that employees are treated fairly and equitably.

two

OFFICE SPACE STANDARDS

The individual worker, seated at his or her desk or worktable, is not only the basic unit of an office, the basic working area which he has completely to himself is the foundation of all space planning and administration. Determining the space allotment for each worker is the beginning of our determination of space standards for the office as a whole; we work in space administration from the individual work station to the over-all plan. If we do not, we're liable to find that quarters have been rented or built that simply won't accommodate all the company's workers.

And, to a degree, the amount of space given each worker reflects the atmosphere of the office as a whole—for individual space allotments can be either economical or liberal. The finished office will more often than not be characterized throughout by the type of thinking first indicated in the determination of individual space standards. Other factors will operate to set space standards, too, of course; in an industrial corporation, where many of the jobs are of a strictly routine character, it is common practice to employ a small or economical space standard for individual workers, although complex operations requiring bulky equipment will usually dictate a more liberal space allotment. In general, in offices where specialized work is done and there are many visitors, or where a strong effort has been made to promote high worker morale, a generous space allotment will be used.

In either instance, determination of the actual working space reserved for each worker, and of the increased amount of space to be given each higher echelon in the company table of organization, is the very first step in scientific space planning. And within our limits of generous and economical individual space standards, certain broad trends for various types of offices can be seen.

Government office space, for instance, like the average large corporation's space for routine clerical positions, will usually be set up on economical standards. Institutional organizations, such as banks, insurance companies, and very large corporations with great numbers of clerical workers, will also tend to use economical space-allotment standards in areas where there is little contact with the public. The reason is obvious: Generous standards in very large organizations mean greatly increased rental or building costs. Smaller offices and more personalized organizations, which do not have great numbers of clerks engaged in routine clerical operations, may profitably use much more liberal standards even on the basic clerical level. And by the same token, the same institutional organizations — banks, insurance companies, etc. — that set compact space standards for their internal processing departments must alter their basic space standards, even for routine workers, in departments where there is a considerable degree of contact with the public.

Before we go any further and discuss particular space allotments appropriate to various types of workers, let's define our terms. Space allotment, as we have said, is the number of square feet required to house a person or a department. But "square feet" itself can mean a variety of different things, can be interpreted in many ways.

To the office manager, "square feet" means the amount of space required to accommodate a desk and a chair, plus a wastebasket, occasional file or bookcase, a departmental or work-row aisle, and, perhaps, a clothes rack. The office manager, in other words, is concerned with "net assignable space." "Square feet" to the architect or building manager means the entire area of a single floor, including building corridors and service facilities, which the office manager often ignores in his reckoning. The former is thinking in terms of net square feet; the latter, in terms of gross square feet.

This may seem to be laboring an obvious point, but the essence of communication is a common agreement on terms, and planning office space is a matter of many points of view being meshed together. Varying use of basic terms can cause confusion in the beginning and bad results in the end. Even such a simple term as "square feet," when used by a variety of people each with a different conception of its meaning, can create a great deal of confusion and trouble. The office manager, as well as top management, is interested in usable office space when discussing assignment of given areas with department heads, with a landlord in rental quarters, or with architect, engineer, or builder during construction. (See Illustration 2-1 for net assignable square feet, gross square feet, etc.) So, to make the

Illus. 2-1. Area study of typical office building space.

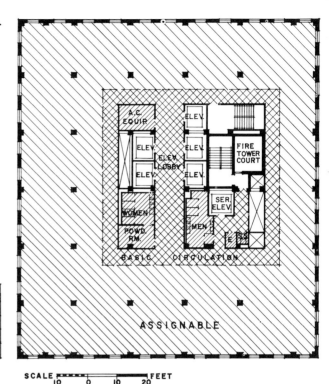

SYMBOL	SPACE	SQ. FT.	% OF RENTABLE
▨	ASSIGNABLE (NET)	7310	77
▩	BASIC CIRCULATION	1660	17
▨	BUILDING SERVICES	530	06
	TOTAL RENTABLE	9500	100%

SCALE ⊢━━━━━┤ FEET
10   0   10   20

various terms used by these latter groups clear, the distinctions between net assignable and gross rentable space should be drawn. To clarify these meanings, we quote from a pamphlet published by The Real Estate Board of New York, *Standard Method of Floor Measuremetn for Office Buildings:*

SINGLE TENANCY FLOORS

Three steps are to be followed to determine the rentable area:
    (a) Compute gross area.
    (b) Deduct certain areas.
    (c) Add applicable share of areas to be apportioned (see paragraph c, below).

(a) *Gross Area:*
    The gross area of a floor shall be the entire area within the exterior walls. If the exterior wall consists in whole or part of windows, fixed clear glass or other transparent material, the measurement shall be taken to the inside of the glass or other transparent material. If it consists solely of a non-transparent material, the measurement shall be taken to the inside surface of the outer masonry building wall.

(b) *Deductions from Gross Area:*
    The following non-rentable building areas with their finished enclosing walls are to be deducted:
    1. Public elevator shafts and elevator machine rooms.
    2. Public stairs.

3. Fire tower and fire tower court.
4. Main telephone and electric switchboard room except:
   (a) where the same is leased by tenant, or
   (b) is a special installation
5. Areas within the gross area which are to be apportioned (see paragraph c, below).

(*Note*: If a base building area to be deducted and a base building area that is rentable have a common wall, the thickness of the wall is to be equally divided; e.g., if an elevator shaft is adjacent to a telephone closet, the elevator shaft and half of the finished dividing wall are to be deducted.

(c) *Areas to Be Apportioned:*

1. Air conditioning facilities: All air conditioning floors and other areas throughout and within the building (exclusive of tenant's special air conditioning facilities) including their finished enclosing walls containing equipment or enclosing pipes, ducts, or shafts serving the facilities are to be apportioned to the areas they serve.

2. Whenever the height of an air conditioning facility room or floor above the grade floor shall exceed the average story height in the building by more than 25%, then the area of such room or floor shall be determined by multiplying the floor area by the percentage that the height of the room or floor exceeds the average story height, and adding the area so determined to the area of the room or floor.

MULTIPLE OCCUPANCY FLOORS

The total of the rentable areas for two or more tenants on a floor shall be the rentable area for that floor as computed in the manner for single tenancy floors, except that public corridors of the floor shall be included.

Three steps are to be followed:

1. Compute the net area for such floor.
2. Compute the net area for each tenant.
3. To determine the rentable area for any tenant, multiply the rentable area of such floor by a fraction whose numerator is the net area for such tenant and whose denominator is the net area for such floor.

(a) *Net Area for Any Floor:*

The net area shall be the gross area as described for single tenancy floors less the entire core areas (including the finished enclosing walls thereof but excluding any part of the core rented to a tenant) and corridors (excluding the enclosing walls thereof).

(b) *Net Area for Each Tenant:*

Exterior walls are to be measured as described in procedure for gross area. Demising walls between tenants are to be equally divided. Corridor walls to the finished corridor side are to be included in the net area of each tenant. (See Illustration 2-2.)

SINGLE TENANCY BUILDINGS

The rentable area of a Single Tenancy Building shall be the aggregate area thereof without any deduction.

GENERAL

Architectural plans when available are to be used. Tenant special installations including, but not limited to, private elevators, stairs, special flues, dumbwaiter shafts and special air conditioning facilities are included within the rentable

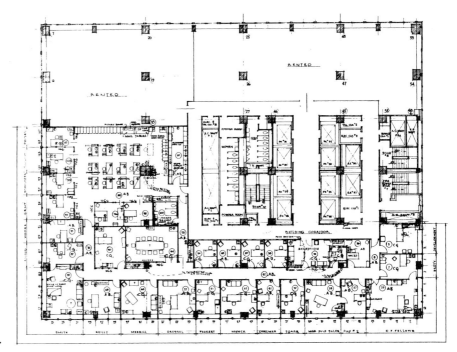

Illus. 2-2. Multiple-occupancy floor.

area of such tenant. In determining whether a floor is, and in computing the aggregate rentable area of, a single tenancy floor, any special installation on said floor of another tenant shall be disregarded. In computing the aggregate rentable area of any multiple occupancy floor, any special installation of a tenant who is not a tenant of any other part of such floor shall be disregarded.

In addition to drawing the distinctions between gross and net square feet, a few other terms which will be used throughout the book should be defined here.

The first is "module." When considering general interior office space, we will be talking about *space modules* and *functional modules*. We will also be talking about architectural, or structural, and mechanical modular design and construction.

To begin at the beginning, module is a "standard or unit of measure" by which the proportions of a building or structure are judged. Adapting this term to the office, a functional module then refers to a unit of space required to perform a specific office function. The module, once adopted, is repeated for every station that must perform that function. When we talk about a private office, we are considering a functional module. And when we use modular space planning, every private office for a certain rank of executive will have the same space. The module for one group may incorporate 200 square feet; it may be set up as 300 square feet. Whatever area is established, it becomes the standard for all private offices for executives at this particular level in the organization.

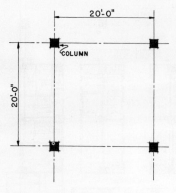

Illus. 2-3. Typical structural bay.

Similarly, in an open general office, we might establish the office worker's functional module as 80 square feet; that is, we would establish as our standard an allotment of 80 square feet for each individual.

Structural modular construction refers, as its name implies, to a structural or architectural unit. When we say that a building is constructed around 20-foot bays, we mean that the supporting columns are spaced 20 feet apart. The structural module for the building is then 20 feet, and the structural bay area is 400 square feet (Illustration 2-3). Under this same condition, the windows on the perimeter of the building might be placed on 10-foot centers, which would divide the 20-foot structural module two times to give us a linear module of 10 feet.

And in the modern office building, the structural module is the end result of the requirements of the functional module, just as the office's total space requirements are dictated by the decision as to how much space is to be given to individual office workers and machines.

We have previously stated that total modularity is the optimum condition of building, wherein furniture and facilities space requirements are integrated with structure for complete flexibility. Heretofore we have thought of building modularity in terms of interior spatial conditioning coordinated with structure to satisfy a private office size. Today, total modularity satifies general office functional planning, as well. This fact is based upon the premise that in planning desk layouts in the open general office areas, we require the occasional panelwall and a ceiling module which coordinates light, sound and air conditioning, and partition attachment.

This brings us back to the starting point: the basic office worker at his or her work station. We have discussed some of the conditions which lead a company to choose liberal or economical space standards or modules for its various levels of employees. What is the range of such standards, the limit beneath which individual work space cannot go, at which it becomes wholly impractical?

Determining the appropriate standards within this range, in terms of the needs and purposes of his company, is the first responsibility of the space administrator in his planning role. It is his responsibility, too, to compromise the functional space modules in existing structures to meet the desired standards, or to develop the proper new space modules for office-space allotments and structure in new construction. Thus he must establish space standards before he makes his recommendation about the total amount of space his company must rent or build in a move to new quarters.

If a new building project is being planned, establishing space standards (within reasonable limits) is fairly simple, since the column ceiling spans and window modules of the building can be designed to satisfy the space-allotment standards finally agreed on. On the other hand, if the office is to be moved into space in an existing building, office space standards may, to a degree, have to be compromised to meet existing space limitations. This problem occurs mainly in private offices, the size of which is often controlled by ceiling modules, column spans, and particularly window modules. Arbitrary insistence on predetermined space standards in some existing structures could mean that two private offices, divided by a partition, would share one window—an obviously ridiculous situation. In the open general office areas the functional office layout plan influenced by furniture and partitions is easily integrated with a newly installed modular ceiling design compatible to panelwall work station dividers.

By using 20 feet by 20 feet as the average structural bay, a variety of private-office standards, all falling within an acceptable range, can be established [see typical exhibits in Illustrations 2-4 and 2-4 (*Cont.*)]:

Type	Dimensions, feet	Area, square feet
A	20 × 20	400
B	10 × 20	200
C	20 × 15	300
D	10 × 15	150

For general office workers, occupying standard 60- by 30-inch desks, we might assign space allotments that are economical at 65 square feet per person or liberal at 80 square feet per person (see Illustrations 2-4 to 2-6). And a supervisor might be assigned 100 square feet.

Twenty-by-twenty structural bays are not the only dimensions possible—other spacing may be used, particularly in general office areas where longer column spans may be necessary or desirable.

Illus. 2-4. Space allotments based on tatus. (*Courtesy of Eggers Partnership.*)

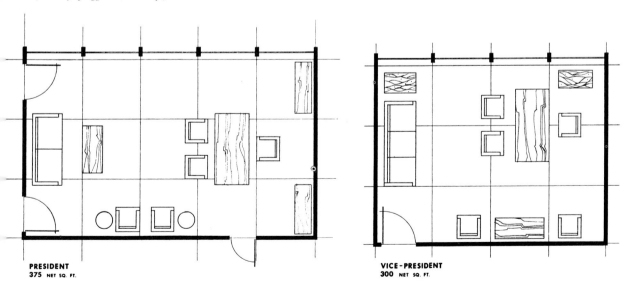

PRESIDENT
375 NET SQ. FT.

VICE-PRESIDENT
300 NET SQ. FT.

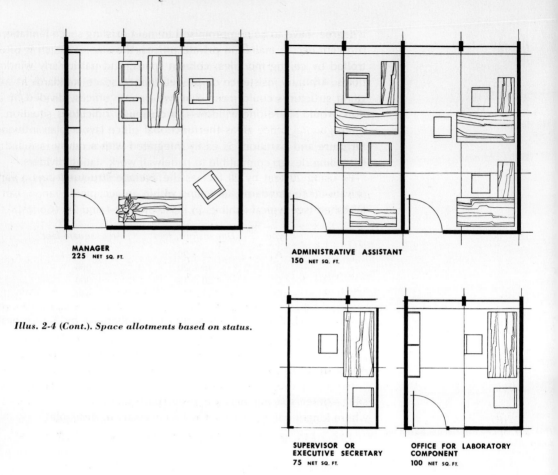

MANAGER
225 NET SQ. FT.

ADMINISTRATIVE ASSISTANT
150 NET SQ. FT.

Illus. 2-4 (Cont.). Space allotments based on status.

**SUPERVISOR OR
EXECUTIVE SECRETARY**
75 NET SQ. FT.

**OFFICE FOR LABORATORY
COMPONENT**
100 NET SQ. FT.

The optimum practicable span for the general office is about 35 feet. Similarly, depending on whether liberal or economical space standards are set for private offices, column spans in such areas might range from 16 to 40 feet. This would permit a wide range of sizes in private offices. But here we must be careful of the ceiling's modularity, as demonstrated in the U.S. Steel Building (see Illustration 7-6) — should we go to a net 4-foot ceiling module with provision for a panelwall or partition at any approximate 4-foot dimension, we would be able to build economically sized inside and outside offices, generally as follows:

Type	Dimensions, feet	Area, square feet
A	16 × 16	256 (approx. 250)
B	12 × 16	192 (approx. 200)
C	12 × 12	144 (approx. 150)
D	8 × 12	96 (approx. 100)

Special office equipment
space-allotment standards, a
space-allotment standards e
ning in order to determine
must be done before gene
ment is not flexible; it wi
cannot be reduced, and
remaining total assignable
accurately planned.

For the same reason, sp
mail, medical services, ca
and service rooms, must
office areas can be firm
space remaining after t
often be the determinin
economical private and

The total space allotted to special areas—acce
service facilities, reception and conference rooms—is calculated first by
estimating space required in new quarters. Then general and private office
individual space standards are multiplied by the number of workers in
each category to be housed. This total square-foot figure added to the first
represents the total net office space required by the organization. Obviously, in moving into an existing office building, the building's present
dimensions will to a degree control the space standards decided on; in
planning a new tenant-owned building, the space standards can be the
starting point, and the building can be constructed to meet the desired
space standards.

Assuming that a company is not constrained by space limitations in an
existing building, is free to set any individual standards that seem desirable, which is better—liberal or economical space standards? What is
the difference, what is the range between liberal and economical standards?

To take the last question first, 100 square feet per general office clerical
worker would be generally considered a liberal standard; 65 square feet an
economical standard. The National Office Management Association (now
the Administrative Management Society) listed in the *NOMA Office Standard—Office Space Assignments:*

1. Scope and Purpose
   1.1 These standards can be used to determine the number of square feet of
       office space required for an office layout.
2. Exceptions
   2.1 The standards mentioned below do not provide for large concentrations
       of file space, storage space, special equipment, and miscellaneous areas,
       as well as building services (elevators, stairs, toilets, electrical and ser-
       vice closets, etc.) and building and general corridors.

2.2 In new buildings, the Standard for private offices contemplates building column structural bay of 20′ × 20′, and windows on 10′ centers.

2.3 In existing buildings, private office allotments might vary with limitations of column spans and window spacing.

3. Office Space Assignment Standards

3.1 The following table of allowances will serve for Standard considerations.

3.1.1 General Office Area—60–80 sq. ft. per person.

3.1.2 Private Office Area

3.1.2.1 Executive Private Office—500 sq. ft.

  (Private Office—400 sq. ft.

  Corridor   —100 sq. ft.)

3.1.2.2 Administrative Private Office—250 sq. ft.

  (Private Office—200 sq. ft.

  Corridor   —50 sq. ft.)

3.2 The above space allotments provide for occasional accessories, files, coat racks, cabinets, water coolers, and such.

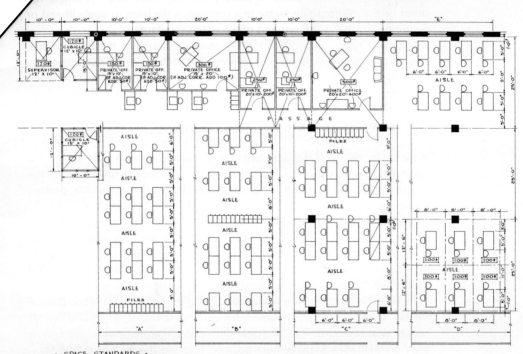

- SPACE STANDARDS -

GENERAL OFFICE AREA = 65# PER PERSON
  CROSS-OVER AISLE EVERY THIRD BAY
  SCHEME "C" DEMONSTRATES THIS.
PRIVATE OFFICE AREAS : EXECUTIVE
  500# (PO. 400# - CORRIDOR 100#)
EXECUTIVE ASSISTANT OR SECRETARY
  250# (PO. 200# - CORRIDOR 50#)
ADMINISTRATIVE EXECUTIVE
  300# (IF ADJACENT CORR. ADD 100#)
ADMINISTRATIVE ASS'T. OR SECRETARY
  150# (IF ADJACENT CORR. ADD 50#)
SPACE ALLOCATIONS FOR PERSONNEL
  RECEIVING VISITORS
  SCHEME "D" = 100# PER PERSON
  SCHEME "E" = 80# PER PERSON
CUBICLE 120# - RAILING OR DWARF PARTITION

- OFFICE SPACE ASSIGNMENT -

SCALE   0 5 10 15 20   FEET

- STANDARD SHEET "B" -
APPROX. 65# PER PERSON USING 60"×34" EQUIPMENT
  " 120# " " FOR SUPERVISOR ·

Illus. 2-5. Graphic office layout of private offices and general office area with an economical space allotment standard of 65 square feet per person, wherein desks abut. Crossover aisles should be provided in every third bay of general office layout.

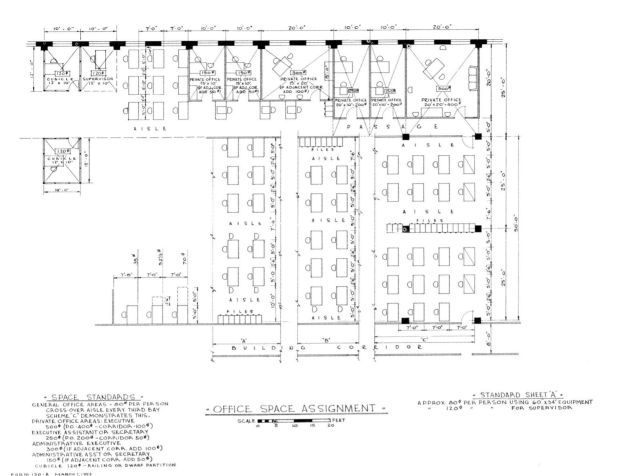

· OFFICE SPACE ASSIGNMENT ·

SCALE
0   5   10   15   20 FEET

· STANDARD SHEET "A" ·
APPROX. 80# PER PERSON USING 60"x54" EQUIPMENT
"   120#   "   "   FOR SUPERVISOR

Illus. 2-6. Graphic office layout of private offices and general office area with a liberal space allotment standard of 80 square feet per person, wherein desks are separated by a minimum of 2½-foot aisles. Crossover aisles should be provided in every third bay of general office layout.

Actual graphics of the above might work out as shown in Illustrations 7-7a, 7-7b, 7-7c.

Now, within the ranges quoted for general office standards, which is better, the upper limit or the lower? We generally recommend, whenever it is feasible, that a generous rather than an economical space standard be used. There are three main reasons for this: Use of generous standards gives a company a built-in expansion factor, improves employee morale, and usually improves employee efficiency and work output as well.

The expansion factor is an obvious benefit of the generous space allotment. A company occupying rented quarters will often find that it is outgrowing in a few short years the quarters it once thought would be adequate for a long period of time. If it has used minimum space standards for workers in its planning and has not reserved expansion space elsewhere in the building, it very often will have to split its office force between two buildings, or move its entire staff into larger quarters. Use of generous standards in the first place gives the company a built-in contraction possibility which gives it expansion space. As it expands, if adjacent space is not readily available in its own building, it can, by reducing its individual space standards, accommodate an increased number of workers without additional space. When more space becomes available in the rental building, it can take another floor or half floor and return to its original generous standards. The company which has stipulated economical standards from the first does not have this time advantage when it needs to house more workers; it must find additional space immediately.

Morale also increases as space allotments are made more generous. Desks separated from, rather than abutting on, each other give each worker more of a sense of pride and prestige in his job, less of a feeling of being part of an assembly line. Moreover, aside from the intangible prestige factor in the workers' minds, a spacious uncrowded office is usually less noisy and more relaxing physically than one that gives an impression of being crowded.

Efficiency, the final argument for generous space standards, is the least obvious of the factors which lead us to urge adoption of the high standards, but it is a very real benefit. When workers' desks are separated, the incidence of gossip, of passing the time of day, of exchanging of confidences, drops noticeably. If desks are separated, one worker has to get up and move to another's desk if he is in the mood for a little casual conversation. Long, personal discussions between two workers are not only more obvious to the supervisor but also more effort for the worker.

Offices that give their workers the benefits of up-to-date individual desks and component needs in adequate space are usually more than compensated for any extra cost involved by an increase in total clerical work output. Furniture and facilities have been found to be 10 per cent and salaries 90 per cent of the office cost.

three

SURVEYING PRESENT SPACE USAGE AND PROJECTING FUTURE REQUIREMENTS

Once space-allotment standards for the new office layout have been decided, it is possible to prepare a formal program of office space requirements. But so far we have been concerned simply with establishing standards for various categories of workers. Now it is necessary for the space administrator to find out just how many of each group of workers there are in the organization, special requirements any of them have that will dictate a compromise in the standards, and any departmental information which will necessitate additional space—over and above individual space allotments for each worker—for departments as a whole.

This is done through a survey of present office space and how it is used, a survey which takes in every office worker—his machines, equipment, and furniture—in the organization and a blueprint of the present office layout.

The survey can be accomplished easily by using analysis forms like the one shown (Illustration 3-1) and a detailed blueprint of present office layout to calculate areas occupied by departments. The analysis forms should be typed, preferably on transparent paper with a reverse carbon backing for use in making additional needed copies. These forms are completed for each department by a liaison person within the department

ANALYSIS SHEET

ORGANIZATION - EQUIPMENT & SPACE

AS OF .... 195......

PRESENT ☐   PROJECTED ☐

PREPARED BY:
KENNETH H. RIPNEN CO., Inc.
ARCHITECTS
OFFICE LAYOUT & OFFICE BUILDING CONSULTANTS
440 4th AVENUE
NEW YORK 16, NEW YORK

JOB No. _____   PAGE _____
DATE: _____
DEPT. SHEET No. ....
OF .... SHEETS

ADDRESS: _____
FLOOR: _____
DEPARTMENT: _____

ROOM NUMBER	DEPARTMENT PERSONNEL		3. NUMBER OF EMPLOYEES			4. PRIVATE OFFICE		5. GENERAL OFFICE			6. SPECIAL AREAS		7. TOTAL AREA	8. EQUIPMENT USED				9. OTHER SPECIAL EQUIP.	10. CONTACT WITH OTHER DEPARTMENTS AND REMARKS
	1.	2. NAME	Male	Female	Total	Square Feet	Pers.	Square Feet	Personnel	Aver.	Square Feet	Pers.	AREA	Desk	Tele-phone	ELECTRICAL MACH. On Desk	Separate		
	JOB TITLE																		

Illus. 3-1. Organization, furniture, and space analysis form.

who works with the space administrator. A department may use as many pages in the forms as it needs to list its requirements, but it is best and simplest to stipulate that two departments cannot be listed on the same page.

Information should be entered horizontally across the form for each individual office worker in each department in the following manner:

Column 1. "Job Title." A job title should be entered for each individual in the department. In the case of secretaries and stenographers, who should be placed close to the executive for whom they work, the job title should include the executive's name—"Secretary to Mr. Jones," or "Stenographer for Mr. White and Mr. Greene." This information can be entered in column 1 or 10.

The room number, if any, should be entered on each line in the left-hand marginal column opposite the jobholder's name to simplify location of individuals and departments.

Column 2: "Name." Each individual in the department should be listed on a separate line; emphasis should be made on accuracy in spelling both job title and name to avoid possible confusion. Personnel of each section and division within the department should be listed together, and three blank lines should be used to separate each divisional group from the next.

The succeeding main-column divisions are each broken into sub-columns for individual information purposes.

Column 3: "Number of Employees"—is divided into three sub-columns, "Male," "Female," and "Total." A check mark in the Male or Female column indicates the sex of the particular employee. The Total column is used only at the bottom of the page to give a final figure for all male and female employees listed on the page; no entry is made, therefore, opposite the individual horizontal listings in this column.

Column 4: "Private Office" has two subcolumns, "Square Feet" and "Personnel." If the individual occupies a private office, the total square feet taken by that office is entered in the first subcolumn. Since "private office" in this context includes an office shared by an executive and his secretary, the number of people actually using the office is entered in the second subcolumn, Personnel. Generally, occupancy of any office area by three or more people will take it out of the private-office category and classify it as general office space.

Column 5: "General Office" is divided into three subcolumns, "Square Feet," "Personnel," and "Average." If the individual occupies general office space, the number of square feet presently occupied will be entered in the first subcolumn. Subcolumns for Personnel and Average are both used for a final total at the end of the listing of the entire department's personnel, so no entries are made at this point.

Column 6: "Special Areas" has as subcolumns "Square Feet" and "Personnel." If the individual being listed works in a special area (file room, storage area, reception room, cafeteria, library, or vault), that fact is indicated by a check in the Personnel column. (Square feet of space given to such special areas are not noted by the department but rather by the space planner.)

Column 7: "Total Area." Whatever square-foot area has been listed for the individual worker in column 4, 5, or 6 is reentered in column 7 for eventual totaling of the entire area occupied by all workers in each department at the close of the listing of department personnel.

Column 8: "Equipment Used" is divided into four subcolumns: "Desk," "Telephone," "Electric Machine on Desk," "Electric Machine Separate." In these subcolumns, code symbols or abbreviations are used for standard equipment, as "D" for a regular desk, "S" for a secretarial or typist's desk, "T" for a table, and "D.T." for a desk-table arrangement. Electric machines, either on the desk or separate from the desk, are listed by abbreviations. This information is necessary to indicate the number of electric outlets needed for the work station.

Under the telephone subcolumn, the number of phones needed by the individual should also be indicated by a 1 or 2.

Column 9: "Other Special Equipment." Such things as files, bookcases, visitors' chairs, etc., needed by the individual worker are listed here.

Column 10: "Contacts with Other Departments." Listed here are the departments other than his own with which the individual worker has most frequent contact and the approximate frequency of such contacts. This will help not only in locating departments which must work closely together in areas convenient to each other but will also aid in placing the individual worker in the particular area of his department where contact with the second department may be made most easily. It will also aid the space planner to estimate on an over-all basis how much traffic must be anticipated within the department and so help him in planning aisles and corridors.

With the completion of this first form by all departments, the company has a complete record of the way its present space is apportioned—the first step for planning future space requirements in a scientific fashion. But continuing expansion of the business, with accompanying expansion of personnel needs, should also be anticipated in any well-designed space study for a modern company. How can such future space needs be anticipated?

Usually the best way to arrive at a reliable estimate of what such needs may be is to poll each department to see just how much a given expansion of the company's business would affect the particular department's space needs. One way of doing this is for the office space administrator to send out a memo requiring each department to estimate how many additional workers or machines it would need if the company's gross annual sales volume were to be increased by $1 million, $5 million, or $10 million, or whatever is appropriate in terms of the company's size. Then, by comparing departmental estimates with top management's own forecasts of the company's probable increase in sales volume over the next five-, ten-, or twenty-year period, some planned and logical provision for expansion space can be made for any given period of years the company chooses to elect.

Normally, when a company rents, builds, or modernizes space for new occupancy, it should plan the original office space on liberal enough standards to be adequate for anticipated personnel expansion during the next five-to-ten-year period. In other words, individual space standards should be set high enough to permit any additional workers that might reasonably be added in such a period to be accommodated by contraction of these standards. In addition, a company should allow for a preplanned expansion factor beyond the ten-year point. In the case of a company constructing its own building, the normal procedure would be to have its building designed in such a way that it could be expanded at some future time by the addition of a new wing or extension or floors. Provision for the new wing or extension would be made in the original design, even though it would not be built for some years after construction of the original building. Thus, when the addition is eventually built, it will be compatible functionally with the original in terms of appearance, interior work flow, and departmental groupings. In the case of rented or modernized space, the preplanned expansion factor, beyond the reserve space built into the first office occupied, can be covered by rental options or by renting adjacent space and then subletting it to other tenants.

These are the principles by which future expansion needs can be anticipated and provided for. Now let us see how these principles are put into action in the space-planning stages. The same space analysis forms used for the survey of existing space are employed to determine future needs. Again each worker in the department is listed, together with the equipment he has and whether he occupies a private office or general office space. But now each department head also lists additional workers he would need for the increased work load based on the projected sales increase that management has determined should be the controlling figure in planning expansion requirements.

Information is entered as to whether these currently nonexistent workers would occupy general or private-office space, what equipment they would need, etc. This is, of course, done solely on the basis of job titles.

The analysis form for projected space also indicates what requirements the department would have for additional special rooms, conference rooms, etc., under the anticipated expansion.

But on this second go round of the space-allotment form, the department liaison person makes one significant omission. He does not enter area figures for the individual space to be occupied by each worker, for the purpose of this second set of figures is determination of the new needs of the company. In determining these new needs, the new individual space allotment per worker decided on by the company will be used as the key factor. Thus the square-foot columns are left blank on the form on its second journey through the departments, and will be filled in subsequently by the space administrator.

The space administrator now goes through these second forms, entering the approved new individual space allotment standards for each grade of worker after each worker's name. He fills in figures, too, for the space requirements for the workers not presently on the staff who would be added if the company were to expand at the anticipated rate.

This completed, the space administrator reviews with each department head the space allotted each of his workers in order to make sure that special cases demanding some compromise with the basic space allotment are covered. The space administrator also studies each department's special areas and enters the figures for the space occupied by them on both sets of forms. Once each department head has had a chance to review his new space-allotment figures for each of the department's workers, the space administrator is ready to go ahead with the next stage of his work. First, however, he has the department head sign a formal approval of the final approved space planning program analysis sheet.

As each analysis sheet, on both the first study of existing space and the second survey of projected space, is completed, the space planner totals the subcolumns of columns 3, 4, 5, and 6 so that he has in summary form at the bottom of each sheet, or at the end of the departmental roster if the last page does not take a full sheet, the total number of male personnel, total number of female personnel, total of all personnel, total square-foot area given to private offices, number of people housed in private offices, total square-feet area given to working space in general offices, and total number of personnel working in general offices.

From these last two general office figures he derives the average number of square feet per worker in general office areas. This, of course, is a gross figure, which will be higher than the individual space-allotment standard set for individual workers in the projected space study, since assignments for different grades of workers will vary between 65 and 100 square feet per person. Thus, even if a space-allotment standard of 65 square feet per general office worker has been determined, the gross average will appear much higher. Since the greatest number of office workers occupy space in the general office area, the gross average here is a control factor which varies from 65 to 80 or 100 square feet per person. Similar totals can be found for special areas, number of telephones, electric machines, etc. Thus space analysis sheets give not only individual information for each person—current and future—listed on each sheet but also summary information for all persons and equipment within each department.

These completed analysis sheets are now reviewed by the entire space-planning committee, if the company has appointed one to work with the space administrator in designing the new office or redesigning the current office. (The constitution of such a company committee will be discussed later in this chapter.) The entire working committee has a chance to approve or disapprove the final departmental totals which have already been checked by the space administrator with each department head. Thus there is a final review by the company of the accuracy and reasonableness of each department's projected needs.

Once the committee has accepted the total space-requirement figures for each department as shown on the survey of projected space, the space administrator, using the totals from the two departmental surveys, begins to prepare his master analysis form—*Summary of Space and Personnel*. This form becomes his working tool in comparing present and projected organization needs in terms of total space and personnel. Major divisions on this form are "Present Location" and "Present and Projected Space Needs" (see Illustration 3-2). Under Present Location are subcolumns "Building" and "Floor." The next subcolumn is "Department." Under both Present and Projected columns, subcolumns are "Personnel"—with provision for entering number of men, number of women, total personnel—and "Total Assignable Area in Square Feet."

The summary totals for each department's present and projected space requirements, arrived at in the original space program forms, are now transferred department by department to the Present and Projected columns of the *Summary of Space and Personnel* form. Now the space administrator has, in summary form, a comparison of present and projected total space and personnel requirements for each department within the organization.

When the summary analysis is finished, it becomes the basic operating guide, the program for the planning of the new office layout, the design of the new office building, the rental of new office space. This is the basic information on the total net space the organization must have to house all its clerical and executive functions. When building corridor space is added to this total figure, the organization knows precisely how many gross square feet of space it needs to house its office organization.

As a check on the accuracy of the projection as to future space needs due to expansion, some larger companies carry out periodic "space audits" after they have occupied the new space for which the expansion factor has been planned. These audits may be done on a monthly basis during the first year in which they are carried out. If expansion needs seem to be falling quite close to the estimates made before the company acquired its new space, the audits may be made quarterly during the second year; then, if estimates and realities still match closely, annually thereafter. In this way, a large company can always foresee possible space problems long enough before they occur to make sure the best and most economical continuous space administration is possible. Incidentally, such

SUMMARY OF SPACE PERSONNEL

AS OF _____ 195___

PREPARED BY:
KENNETH H. RIPNEN CO., Inc.
ARCHITECTS
OFFICE LAYOUT & OFFICE BUILDING CONSULTANTS
440 4th AVENUE
NEW YORK 16, NEW YORK

JOB NO.

PAGE

DATE:

PRESENT LOCATION		DEPARTMENT	PRESENT					PROJECTED					REMARKS
BUILDING	FL.		PERSONNEL			TOTAL ASSIGNABLE AREA SQ. FT.		TOTAL ASSIGNABLE AREA SQ. FT.	PERSONNEL				
			M	F	TOTAL				M	F	TOTAL		

Illus. 3-2. Personnel and space summary form.

audits also reveal unanticipated free space in any department when personnel is reduced. This may be called into use if needed. So the audits not only serve the purpose of checking to see whether expansion needs have been accurately estimated but also furnish a running control on current space allotments within departments. They are carried out on the same space-analysis forms used in the basic present and projected space surveys.

Earlier in the chapter it was mentioned that the space administrator, after checking his projected space figures with department heads, reviewed his over-all departmental space allotments with a space-planning committee composed of organization representatives. While such a committee is not always essential in planning space assignments, forming a committee is one of the best and most direct methods of checking every phase of the space-planning program. Committee members can bulwark the projected space needs shown on the summary analysis, check on the accuracy of expansion needs cited by department heads, generally create support for the whole space-planning program, and also certify the work for submission to top management and higher authority for any proposed action on office space.

1802818

There are times when the space administrator makes no contact with department heads in arriving at space requirements of a company, other than asking them to fill out analysis forms showing present usage and projected needs. This happens when a company is considering renewal of leases, move of offices (urban or suburban), expansion or modernization of its office building, and ventures which may or may not happen.

In these instances, the space-analysis forms are sent to department heads, graphic space standards are agreed upon in committee, and forms are posted in committee to establish space requirements for actions under consideration.

The make-up of a typical departmental committee to work with the space administrator in all space projections might be as shown in Illustration 3-3. This suggested departmental representation might be either expanded or reduced, according to the size, scope, and number of departments within the company. There are three major considerations that should be the guiding factors in setting up any space-planning committee, and they are really more important than the precise departmental representation on the committee. They are:

1. The committee chairman should have a wide knowledge of the company and its procedures as well as its equipment and its specialized needs. It is essential that his approach to problems be objective. Only if he has these qualities can he function well as a coordinator and mediator between factions, for there are bound to be divergent opinions among the departments as to the importance of each department's stated space needs.

2. Each representative on the committee must be an authority in his

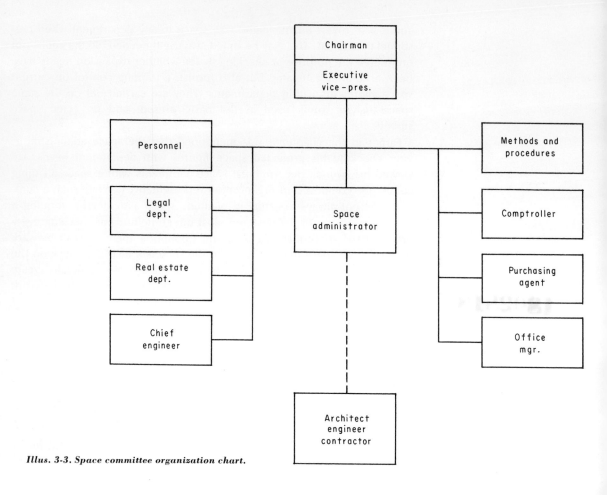

Illus. 3-3. Space committee organization chart.

own functional field so that he will be qualified to present its needs accurately and completely. He should also have enough general knowledge of the work of other departments to be able to evaluate their stated needs fairly and accurately.

3. Each representative should be of high enough rank or enjoy sufficient confidence within his department to be able to make decisions and agreements on behalf of the department. Sometimes the architect, engineer, or contractor serves on the space-planning committee as an outside consultant, just as a lawyer, accountant, or public relations man may serve on other company committees.

An advantage of the committee system which is not to be overlooked is the fact that it exploits some very human tendencies for the good of the organization as a whole. Each party to a mutual agreement, since he is bound by it, becomes a defender of that agreement, either consciously or unconsciously.

There are, of course, disadvantages as well. Committees are often slow in arriving at decisions, and their deliberations can often be frustrating to the point of exasperation on the part of all. The chairman, unless he has really superior organizing and directing ability, will often run out of ways to speed the committee's work. Personality clashes do creep in despite the most careful planning and guidance, and obviously, when various departments' space needs are being evaluated, the ever-present fact of interdepartmental overlapping of functions and responsibilities is going to create some problems.

By and large, however, for a company establishing a new space program, the committee form of organization will still give the best results and aid the office space administrator in the endorsement of his recommendations, standards, and objectives. The slowness of action is offset by a great deal of free publicity within the organization and acceptance of the value of space planning by all parts of the organization. Results of the space-planning program will be accepted in better faith by all worker levels if a representative committe has reviewed each step in the program. Moreover, after the entire space-planning program has gained momentum, certain members of the committee may prove ideal timber with which to build a smaller but faster-moving space-administration committee. This committee would be responsible for continued maintenance and control of the space program after the space allocations have been put into effect in the new office, and would recommend to management continued upgrading and betterment of standards.

Now that our space administrator has guided his program through the preliminary stages of analysis of present space, computation of required new space, review by the committee, and approval of final summary of total space needed to house the organization as it exists now and as it may exist in the future, he has his over-all figures and dimensions. He knows how much total space will be needed by individual workers, by departments, and by the organization as a whole. He is ready to proceed to his next step: the planning of departmental locations in relation to each other in the projected reallocation of space in a new building or modernization.

four

CHARTING THE ORGANIZATION
AND ANALYZING
WORK RELATIONSHIPS
AND WORK FLOW

In order to plan layouts, knowledge of organization structure, work relationship of departments and individuals is basic to office layout planning. This is obviously one of the most vital steps in the entire space-planning program, and it requires both care and a thorough working knowledge of the organization on the part of the space administrator. A good method of visualizing the problem to be faced and solved is to start by making a graphic chart of the organization as it exists and operates and as proposed. Such a basic chart can be made up from the information already gathered in the analysis, or it can be based on the company's own organization chart. Such an organization chart shows the departmental units grouped in their administrative relationship and thus clarifies the basic administrative channels of the company.

WORK-FLOW RELATIONSHIPS

But, of course, an organization chart alone is not enough to show the actual major work-flow pattern of the organization—the processing stream that takes papers, reports, information from one department to another. In order to learn this pattern, the space administrator sits down and reviews with each department head the actual work pattern of his department, where the major paper flow arrives from and where it goes after his department has done its work, has performed its steps in the processing sequence. All this is recorded by the space administrator, becoming part of the vital store of information on which his final office layout plan will be based.

It should be emphasized here that the space administrator takes on none of the characteristics of a systems consultant; he does not make suggestions for improvements in the systems but only in the physical work-flow pattern. Systems are not his business. It is his business to determine what the company's present routines are, what operating system does exist, and then to build his space relationships in accordance with that system to aid it in operating smoothly, with as little lost time and motion as possible. Thus, if Department B receives most of the papers on which it works from Department A and, in turn, after performing its part in the processing cycle, sends those papers on to Department C, it would usually make most sense to place those departments in the same physical sequence as the work flow itself. The same principle applies, of course, to arrangement of mechanical processing equipment within the department. Space requirements of Departments A, B, and C suggest floor sizes.

There are, of course, many different work flows of paper and people in any organization. By graphically representing all these major movements on a chart, the relative importance of each intradepartmental work relationship can be visualized.

Armed with the information he has gained from all department heads, the space administrator now makes his first move toward actual graphic representation of the new office-space plan. A clear plastic overlay is placed over the organization chart. On this overlay, the major work-flow pattern of paper work in the office is indicated between the departments represented on the organization chart. Through the pattern thus revealed, the major work relationships existing between all departments of the organization, and their relative importance, can be determined by the space administrator — a vital step toward intelligent over-all space assignment and office layout planning.

What the space administrator is actually doing when he prepares his overlay on the basic organization chart is making a picture of the company as a dynamic entity. He is creating blueprints of the organization as it actually works rather than as a formal, static, boxed plan of departments in their administrative relationships. He is making rough working drawings of a machine — drawings which not only show the parts of the machine but also make clear how those parts interact with each other. As such, he is drawing the basic plan of his eventual office layout, too, for the good office layout represents in concrete form the working relationships of the organization using it. The good office layout, then, could be likened to the physical elements of a machine, the people to be housed in that office being the energy which drives the machine. Just as in a machine energy can be channeled to produce the best possible results.

Good office work flow and work relationships are the invisible needs of the office and the physical modularity, the architecture, and the engineering elements of the building should combine to meet these needs.

five

PRINCIPLES OF
OFFICE LAYOUT PLANNING

The space administrator now has the two fundamentals for his final office layout plan: the total area required by each department and the working relationship of each department to all other departments in the company. These are his guides to the requirements and thus to the ultimate physical location of departmental working areas. The elements from which the final plan will emerge are complete. But before the final plan itself is made, there are other factors—or rather alternatives—that must be taken into account, evaluated, and finally decided on.

One of the first decisions that must be made by the space adminsistrator and management is the basic space principle to be followed in laying out each departmental general office. Shall an open *integrated* or conventional *compartmented* office layout plan be followed? What is the difference between the theories expressed by the two terms?

Basically, the theory of integrated space calls for open general office areas with a minimum of partitioning, of either the fixed floor-to-ceiling or movable screen type. This type of plan is gaining many adherents today, since it generally offers more flexibility, economy of space, easier worker supervision, and equality of facilities for all parts of the office in comparison with the older, more conventional compartmented layout of office space in which partitions are used to create custom-built departmental units.

For example, in a conventional office occupying 15,000 square feet of space, one might have a sales department of 150 people. The 150 office workers handle sales of eight different products. Each of the eight product sections could have varying numbers of partitioned offices for executives, assistants, and secretaries, as well as special partitioned areas for section office personnel. In this case, the 15,000 square feet of office space housing the eight sections would be composed of a tailor-made layout of eight planned units. If expansion or contraction were necessary in any one of the units, the entire area might have to be rearranged (see Illustration 5-1).

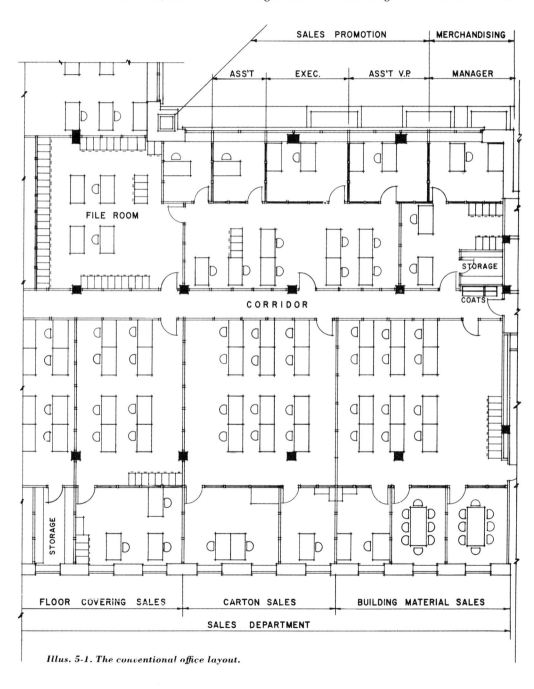

Illus. 5-1. The conventional office layout.

Here is where modularity in office furniture, partitions, and structural and mechanical elements of the building provides a standard so that changes to the plan are made with preplanned tools and are done by in-house staff or custodial help.

Putting this same sales department in an integrated office layout—an open plan—offsets most of the problems, work interruptions, and costs involved if changes become necessary. Assuming that the general office area has been planned so that a line of private offices and a departmental corridor border it, increases or decreases of personnel in any of the eight product sections can be made simply by switching occupants of private offices and adding or removing work stations and screen partitions or panelwalls in the open general office area (see Illustration 5-2).

Any necessary space rearrangement can be performed over a weekend, and the only physical changes in facilities ever necessary under the open plan are restricted to such minor adjustments as occasional changes in underfloor-duct electric and telephone outlets.

Though the open office plan is still more popular with space planners, administrators, and others concerned with space administration than it is with executives reared in the more conventional compartmented office, executives' objections to the open plan can usually be overcome by pointing out these major advantages.

The open integrated space arrangement carries certain conditions, which is one of the reasons the choice between an open integrated and conventional compartmented plan must be made early in the office-planning program. The general office area in an open integrated office layout must be well and uniformly lighted; it requires continuous underfloor ducts for telephone and electric outlets and provisions for mechanical ventilation or air conditioning and sound conditioning. The space should be of a shape to permit convenient access between executive offices and the particular segments of the general office for which each executive office occupant is responsible.

A modular ceiling integrating light, sound, air conditioning, and partitioning through a grooved suspension system is always installed in the closed compartmented approach, whereas a ceiling with no relationship to screens is sometimes installed in the open office. It must be remembered that the closed compartmented office and the panelwall, as well as screens, can work with modular ceilings but not with disassociated ceilings.

Given these conditions, the open integrated office layout can offer all the advantages of the specially partitioned, custom-built office without the disadvantages of compartmented space. Where physical separation by a wall is necessary or justified, movable partial-height partitions, screens, and panelwall are used within the open general area. Continuous-strip underfloor ducts permit placement of electric outlets or telephone outlets at frequent enough intervals along the duct to allow flexibility in desk

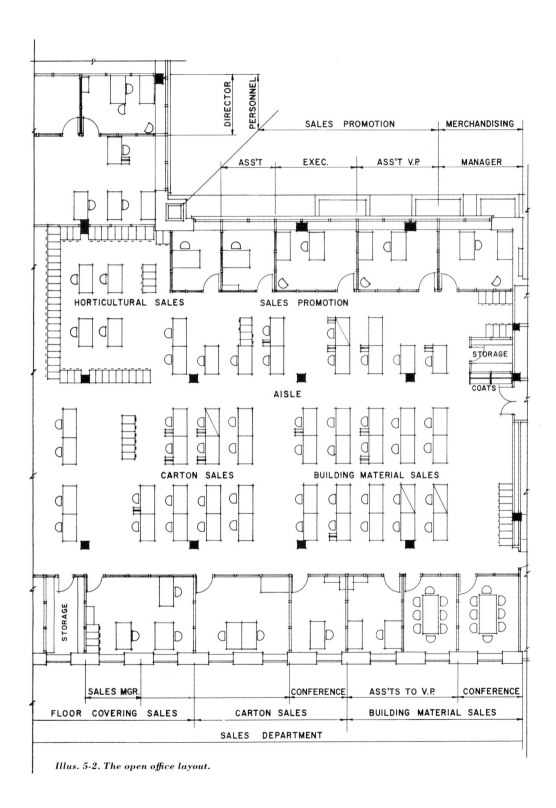

Illus. 5-2. The open office layout.

arrangement. Moreover, such open arrangements permit continuous-strip, or modular overhead lighting layouts within each structural module and regularly spaced air-conditioning strips or grills or perforated ceiling for air-supply and return. These are possible, yet not new, because the absence of interior walls makes specially designed lighting patterns and air-conditioning ducts unnecessary. Thus the open general plan is simpler than the closed compartmented plan; its flexibility in terms of rearrangement of work stations is further assured by the fact that changes in departmental lines affecting office plans require no changes whatever in structural, physical, and mechanical features. Noise level must be kept low—loud voices, machine noise, and visual disorders are the greatest disadvantage.

Now, in the ideal situation, where a new building is to be constructed for the exclusive use of one company, final architectural considerations can be based on the choice of interior-space arrangements as specified by the space administrator. Placement of columns, framing, location of doors and windows, and ideal underfloor-duct, overhead-lighting, air-conditioning and acoustic ceiling arrangements can be worked out with the architect in terms of the basic interior requirements. These elements are further coordinated with office and building services and the basic circulation pattern.

While the same freedom to create the open or conventional office does not exist in rental space, at least underfloor ducts, overhead lighting, sound conditioning, and air-circulation ducts can be installed on the continuous or modular patterns cited for general office areas, as in tenant-owned buildings.

six

CREATING
OFFICE LAYOUT PLANS

With the decision between using closed compartmented or open integrated space patterns made, it is possible for the space administrator to begin to work out the schematic plan (block area layouts) and location of departments and even the interior arrangement of facilities within each department, whether he is working with present or proposed commercial office building space or a situation where the company will construct its own building. In working with existing space, he knows his architectural limitations—the actual physical dimensions of each floor, the column- and window-module interruptions, the placement of the building-service facilities, etc.—and will have to plan around these. In working in terms of a building to be constructed to meet the precise needs of the company, he has, of course, a much freer hand. But in either event, unless he is dealing with rental quarters in an existing building embodying unusually difficult architectural features, he has freedom to use enough space for each of his departments, to locate them in the best and most efficient arrangement relative to each other, and to use open or conventional space planning for his general office areas.

Now begins a process of continuous refinement in creating the final office layout plan, of working from one over-all layout to each specific departmental layout, constantly improving the one by checking it against the other and then reversing the process. At this point we recognize that computer layout planning is scientific and objective, whereas it has been

...perienced that company executives justifiably inject personal ideas in functional office layout planning that are contrary to objectivity.

Let's take it in graphic terms. Let's say our space administrator is working with rented quarters in a conventional rectangular office building which has a perimeter of private offices and a center core of service facilities surrounded by a corridor. A second corridor extends around the perimeter of the building, separating the private offices lining the outside walls from the interior general office open areas. These general office areas are again separated from the service core by the interior building corridor (see Illustration 6-1).

Illus. 6-1. Section from window wall to building core of the Empire State Building (part plan).

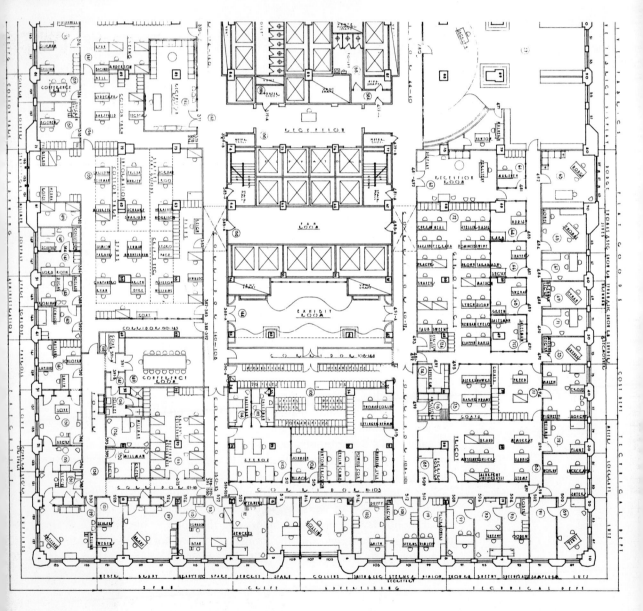

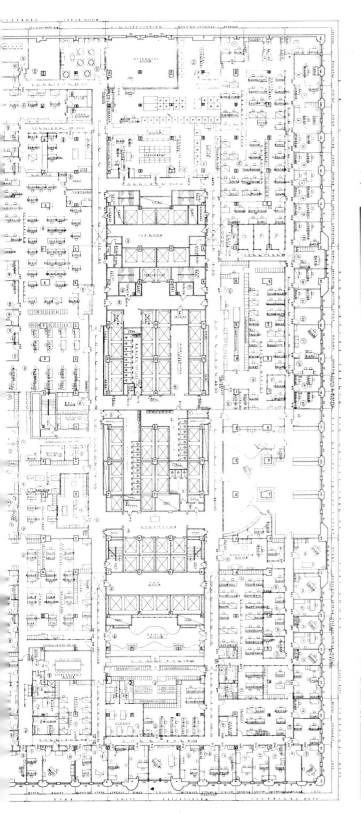

Illus. 6-1 (Cont.). Full floor plan and building photo of the Empire State Building.

Our space administrator would begin by sketching a schematic (block area) diagram of his general departmental areas. The private-office space would for the moment be ignored; that is, to a degree, frozen anyway since the existing construction of the building has often dictated a row of private offices of given area around the building's perimeter. (If however, such space is not needed for private offices but is needed for general office areas, general office space can be extended to the exterior building wall simply by omitting the partition walls between the perimeter private offices.) The point remains that it is the total periphery and interior space with which the space administrator is primarily concerned.

He has from his space-summary sheets the program showing the over-all area requirements in square feet for each department in the organization and their adjacencies. From his charts of the organization structure and work flow, he has knowledge of the direction and flow pattern of the paper work the office exists to handle. Armed with these he blocks out his first departmental grouping on his over-all layout plan, assigning each department the number of square feet shown by his projected space-summary sheets. Thus each department, right from the beginning, incorporates its own expansion space, since it will be remembered that total department space requirements under the projected plan included provisions for the additional workers that might be needed in situations of company expansion.

This first pattern is not a final precise arrangement, but it is a schematic and is accurate in terms of sufficient space for each department and proper functional placement of each departmental area (see Illustration 6-2).

Illus. 6-2. Schematic line drawing layout. (Right) First floor. (Celanese Corporation of America, Charlotte, N.C.)

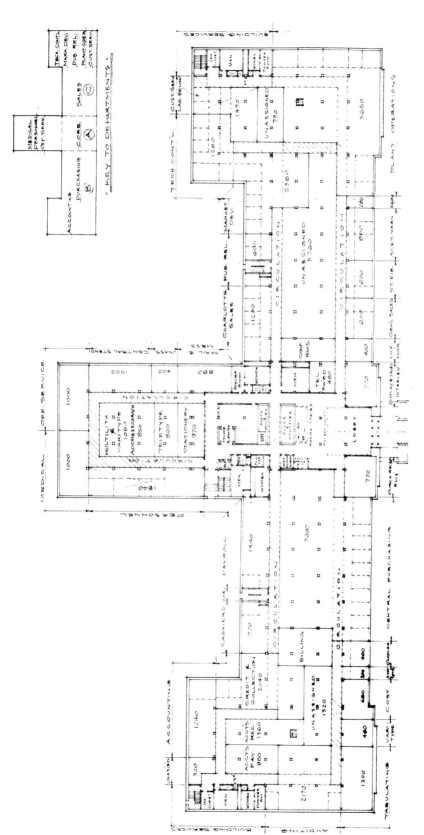

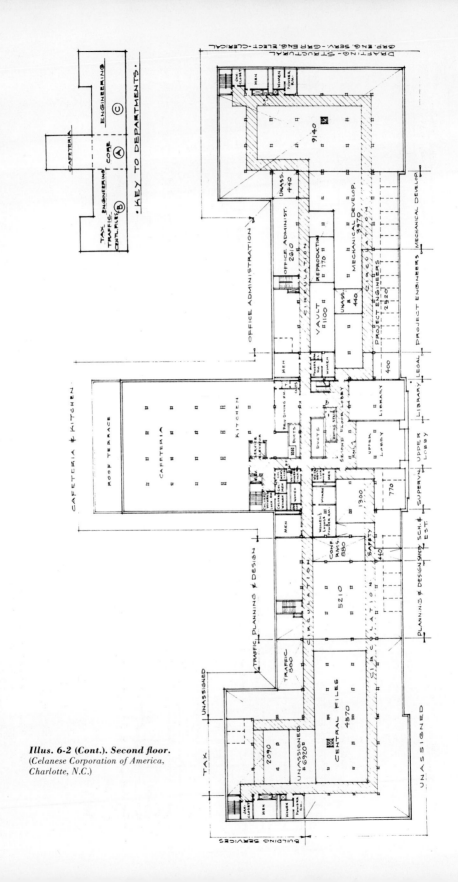

Illus. 6-2 (Cont.). Second floor.
(Celanese Corporation of America, Charlotte, N.C.)

Now it can be refined by a first planning of the interior arrangements of each department. This individual department preliminary space plan is carried out on a fairly detailed basis, actually showing the location of each desk and each piece of free-standing equipment in the general office area (see Illustration 6-3).

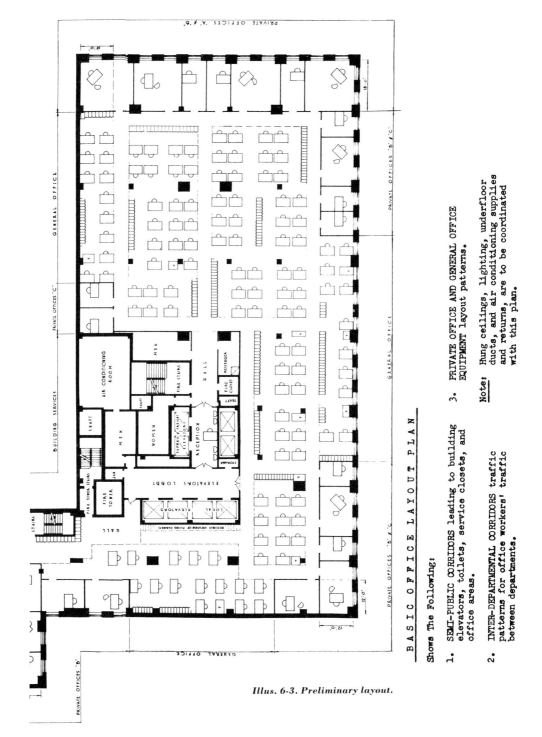

BASIC OFFICE LAYOUT PLAN

Shows The Following:

1. SEMI-PUBLIC CORRIDORS leading to building elevators, toilets, service closets, and office areas.

2. INTER-DEPARTMENTAL CORRIDORS traffic patterns for office workers' traffic between departments.

3. PRIVATE OFFICE AND GENERAL OFFICE EQUIPMENT layout patterns.

Note: Hung ceilings, lighting, underfloor ducts, and air conditioning supplies and returns, are to be coordinated with this plan.

Illus. 6-3. Preliminary layout.

The basic working tool in further detail planning can be the template layout. The template, or actual, model-office layout consists of an outline plan of the proposed space done on paper or cloth. It is prepared on a scale of ¼ inch to the foot and is mounted on a composition board, so that cardboard symbols or actual models representing desks, machines, files, chairs, etc. can be attached to it in various arrangements. These cardboard symbols or models are tiny reproductions of the office's furniture and equipment done on the same ¼ inch to the foot scale (see Illustrations 6-4 and 6-5 — templates and model). The model layout shows the partitions and equipment in three dimensions.

Working with such exact physical symbols, done to precise scale, the best possible interior arrangements for each general office area can be worked out by a process that considers various possibilities until the one best arrangement has been found. Moreover, the template forms a graphic

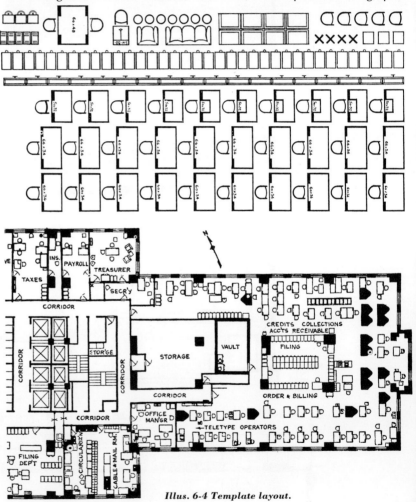

Illus. 6-4 Template layout.

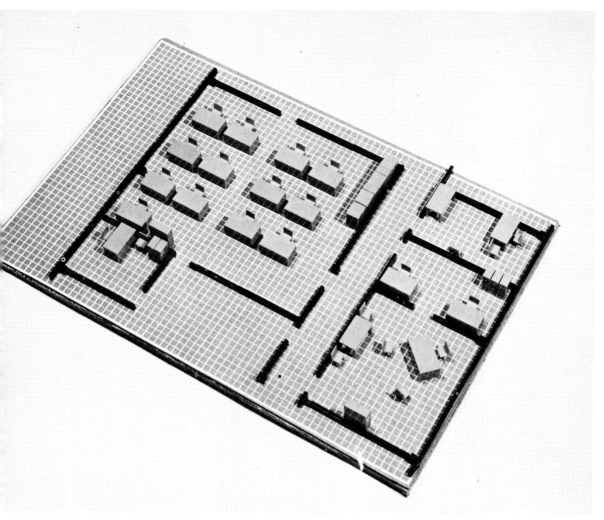

Illus. 6-5. Model office layout.

representation which both space administrator and department head can use and understand equally well. It can also be photographed or photostated for wider distribution and comment in the organization. Thus others in the company can bring forward any criticisms they find for the projected plan, in terms of either individual department requirements or over-all circulation patterns. When space administrator and department head have agreed on the best possible arrangement of equipment and machines, the symbols representing each unit are tacked in place. Various colors of template and models are used to distinguish between existing equipment and new equipment specified under expansion or equipment-replacement plans. The space administrator can now insert names of departments, sections, desk occupants, and special equipment (see Illustration 6-6).

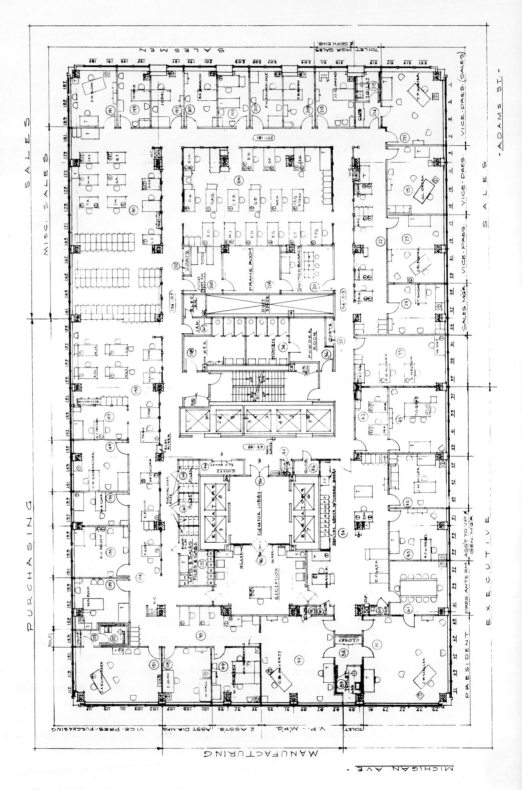

Illus. 6-6. Detail office layout. (*Pullman-Standard Car Manufacuring Co.*)

Partitions are indicated by strips of paper or plastic cut to scale, bearing the symbol of the type of partition to be used. As each template or model layout is completed, it is checked back against the over-all departmental grouping plan for the office as a whole. Although the first over-all plan assigned each department the total space it needed according to the summary sheets, minor adjustments may have to be made at this stage on the departmental dividing lines. Perhaps some features of the building, such as columns, windows, and door placement, make it absolutely imperative to give one department 100 more square feet than it was first thought it would need in order to make workable interior layouts of the department. Such adjustments can now be made on the over-all plan, extending the department area.

The controlling factor for the width of perimeter private-office space is the building-column structure and window module. Assuming the building is built on 20-foot bays, the basic private office on the building perimeter would be bounded by a square of 20 feet. However, within these dimensions many different space arrangements are possible. The president of the company, the executive vice-president, and other officers might have offices 20 feet deep by 30 feet long. Other top-management executives might have offices 20 by 20. Middle management might have offices placed two to a bay, or 10 by 20 feet, or other dimensions which can be fitted within the 20-foot square.

We have already pointed out that wherever private offices are unnecessary, general office areas can be extended to the exterior building wall simply by taking down the partition walls separating perimeter offices in existing space. But even where private offices are necessary around the entire perimeter of the building, they still offer some flexibility in terms of expanding general office space. Let's say our perimeter column span is 20 feet. That means our first line of interior columns inside the building walls will be 20 feet from the exterior wall of the building. Now, assuming we want a corridor separating our interior general offices from our perimeter private offices, we have the choice of placing this corridor *between* the first interior columns and the building wall or on the other side of the first line of interior columns, between columns and general office space. In the first instance, our exterior offices, assuming we stipulate a 5-foot corridor would be established at a 15-foot depth; in the second, they would be a full 20 feet deep. Varying width of this corridor will, of course, control the depth of the private offices bordering it (see Illustration 6-7).

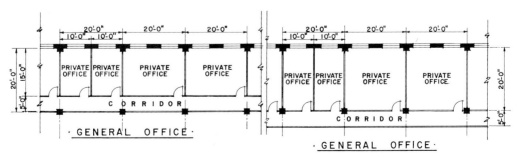

Illus. 6-7. Private-office corridor locations.

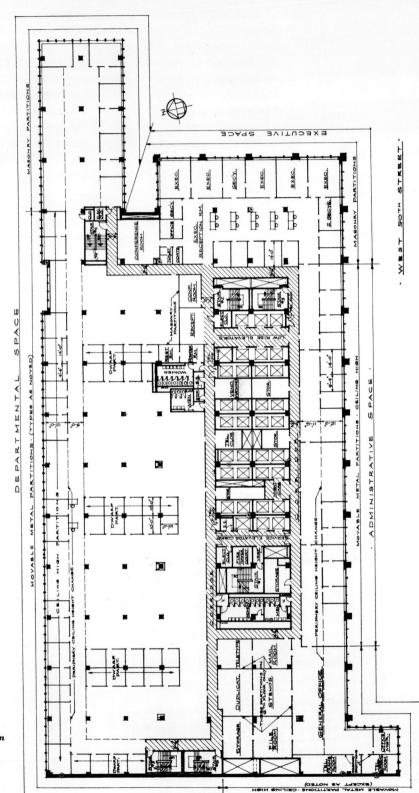

Illus. 6-8. Basic circulation pattern and space disposition plan.

More important than the dimensions of the private offices, however, is the comparative flexibility such placement of corridors gives us in our total interior space. By cutting down on the size of exterior perimeter offices, we add a 5-foot strip along all sides of our interior general office areas.

Thus, even within the comparative rigidity of rental space in a conventional building—provided enough space has been acquired to meet the total demands shown on the summary sheets—a certain degree of flexibility in arrangements is still possible to take care of individual adjustments that must be made as the detailed department-layout requirements are prepared; again this demonstrates the necessity of being prepared to compromise individual space standards to make more space available when needed.

Naturally, in a rental arrangement, as in construction of one's own building, the possible future expansion needs beyond the built-in expansion factor planned for each department of the company must be taken into account. In rented city quarters, this may mean that *all* space foreseen as possibly necessary at some time in the future will have to be acquired at the time of the first move. What happens to this unused space during the long interval in which it is not needed? The most common arrangement is to sublet it on short-term lease to other smaller concerns. In this way, provided the duration of the sublease is kept short enough, the space can always be brought back into the corporation's general space within a reasonable time from the moment when it is first seen that it will be needed.

Another useful tool in creating the office layout plan is the basic circulation pattern and space disposition plan shown in Illustration 6-8.

It goes without saying that at the time the final detailed layouts are made of the new office, layouts should also be prepared showing how departments would shift in any foreseen future expansion into new space reclaimed from a subtenant.

ARCHITECTURAL AND
ENGINEERING INFLUENCES
ON OFFICE LAYOUT
PLANNING

The office building in which structural, physical, and mechanical elements are truly coordinated to serve office functions is, of course, the ideal. Every structure is not a tenant-owned building, however, and therefore cannot — in its original state — meet this ideal fully for each tenant. This doesn't imply that the tenant can't do a great deal to condition space in an existing building for the exact needs of his office. Such conditioning, however, means precise architectural and engineering design and meticulous coordination of the structural, physical, and mechanical elements of the office to contribute to the over-all efficiency of the space arrangement.

The reader's first reaction may be that these elements seem to have little to do with layout. The truth is that they have everything to do with it; they actually can be used to control it and influence the use of space.

Since structural, physical, and mechanical elements — column span, window module, underfloor-duct system, air-conditioning, ceiling suspension system arrangements, height of hung ceilings, lighting pattern — all control layout, the objectives of the layout must be kept in mind when these elements are planned.

How do these elements influence layout?

We have already discussed the distinction between open integrated and conventional compartmented space, citing the former plan as one in which general office areas are left open, with a minimum of ceiling-height partitioning. The open integrated space approach is the one that has been gaining most favor with companies today. But there are two schools of thought about the open integrated space approach. Each of these schools employs the auditorium principle in which general office areas are left open and any necessary divisions are provided by screens and low movable partitions or furniture groupings. It is in the coordination of structural, physical, and mechanical elements with layout that the two schools differ.

One school disregards these elements in such a way as to give almost complete layout freedom: desks, screens, electric and telephone connections, and machines can be placed almost anywhere in the office area. The other employs structural, physical, and mechanical elements in such a way that, although there is great layout flexibility, there is not absolute freedom. The second school in effect freezes the number of possible layouts that may be made by the way in which it uses or locates underfloor ducts, lighting fixtures, hung-ceiling breaks, and air supply and return grills or modular design. The distinction between the two schools is represented by the basic mechanical module selected to condition the space.

Let's say we are faced with a large open area in which we are to establish our general office space. We are prepared to condition that space in terms of the type of office we wish to create. Depending on how we condition it, we can provide our future office with absolute flexibility in placement of dwarf partitions, desks, and machines. Alternatively, we can give it a considerable degree of flexibility—but flexibility which can be expressed only through a certain number of basic office layout patterns.

Perhaps the simplest way to illustrate the difference between the two approaches is offered by the underfloor-duct arrangement. Desks need telephone and electric connections. Our choice as to arrangement of mechanical elements—in this instance the underfloor telephone and electric ducts—of the office determines whether that office is to have complete flexibility in future desk arrangements or is to have only relative flexibility. If we wish complete flexibility, we will use a grid-type underfloor-duct system in which ducts cross each other at regular intervals. In this system, desks can be located anywhere because one can tap in an outlet for telephone or electricity anywhere. If we wish relative flexibility, we will use continuous, parallel underfloor ducts spaced at regular intervals. In this system, desks can be located only above the duct locations providing outlets.

Some offices have placed their basic module in a grid pattern as low as 4 feet. It is also possible to use a corrugated deck floor in which electric or phone connections may be made at almost any point. Such absolute flexibility is not only expensive, it offers, to our mind, positive disadvantages, since complete mobility is simply an invitation to all concerned to place their desks wherever they please, the ultimate of the open office. If the office worker can place office equipment anywhere he wishes on a 4-foot square, you can be sure everyone will want to do it in a different way.

If, on the other hand, underfloor ducts do not form a grid but rather are placed in parallel continuous rows, with a 5-, 8-, or 10-foot interval between each duct, a degree of influence and control through mechanical means is automatically placed on the layout arrangement of the office. Desks must be immediately above or on one side or the other of the duct which carries power, phone, and intercom lines. They cannot be placed anywhere on a square module, or anywhere on the floor area, as they can when a grid or corrugated-deck system is used. In addition to offering a means of control of layout planning, the use of continuous parallel ducts is less expensive than either the grid system or the corrugated-deck arrangement in terms of over-all costs for complete floor construction.

All these factors must be considered when an office layout plan is created, because the decisions taken then on how to condition the proposed space structurally, physically, and mechanically will, as we have shown, have a definite influence on the workability, efficiency, and flexibility of the office layout plan. The decisions made at this point will serve to control the amount of space required as well as the way the space is used.

Whether existing space is to be used or new space is to be built, all these factors are within the control of the office space administrator. Space in a building twenty or thirty years old can be mechanically conditioned in terms of underfloor ducts, light, and air-conditioning and ceiling suspension system patterns to match the best and most modern standards.

Let's look a little further into this concept of influencing office layout planning by structurally, physically, and mechanically conditioning space in the planning stage. After we have achieved in general terms our one best floor layout plan, we can begin to plan the manner in which we will condition our space. Now the over-all office layout plan of furniture and partition standards will serve as the framework for all the structural, physical, and mechanical installations in the space to be occupied.

If the location of corridors is coordinated at this stage with the location of the main supply and return air-conditioning duct, which must run through the office, then hung ceilings can be planned beneath the air ducts, since corridors do not require as much ceiling height as general office space. Such hung ceilings over corridors, running parallel with the perimeter rows of private offices, begin to give the office a point of control of layout, a physical break between types of office space. Together with window modules and column centers, they establish a pattern for planning the exact dimensions and locations of partitions and desks. Thus we see the beginning of control of space through structural and physical elements—the window module and column span and hung-ceiling breaks. The ceiling lighting, air-conditioning grid, and acoustical ceiling panel suspension system introduce coordinated modularity.

If the location of the supply and return grills for air conditioning, the underfloor ducts, and the lighting fixtures in the ceilings are coordinated with the window modules, the column spacing, and the projecting breaks established by hung ceilings over corridors, then the location, type, and size of the partitions defining perimeter private offices are almost established for the planner in terms of the number of private offices possible and the basic private-office space allotment that has already been decided on. There will be a logical pattern of partitions and doors to give private offices of the right size. Almost any other pattern of office layout will be obviously illogical, and here is where compromises to functional office layout planning must be made to preserve the benefits of control through integration and modularity in structure.

By the same token, in general office areas coordinating the intervals between continuous-strip underfloor ducts with the planned location of desks will, as we have shown, serve to control the placement of work stations after the office force has moved in.

The result of integration of all structural, physical, and mechanical elements in terms of the basic office layout plan means that the office can face a future in which it need never fear major alterations every time partitions must be moved to satisfy department or organizational changes. Extensive alterations are not necessary in the physical or mechanical elements even when major office reorganizations are made.

To take a typical example of conditioning space to adapt it to a desired general layout plan, let's assume a company plans to move into rented space in a conventional city skyscraper. Assume that our hypothetical building has a rectangular shape, with building services at the core. The space rented is the area extending from the core to the outer building walls.

Let's assume further that our building is constructed on approximately 20- by 20-foot structural bays and that we intend to establish our own underfloor-duct, lighting, air-conditioning, and hung-ceiling patterns on the single floor into which our office is to be moved. Our total rented space is in accord with the required space already established by our survey of projected space requirements.

Our first step would be to establish the basic access and circulation pattern that would give our office maximum usefulness and flexibility. We would lay out our semipublic corridor, giving access to all net usable space, with room number and area by room.

In a conventional building of the type we are using as an example, the semipublic basic corridor would usually form a rectangle separating the building-service core from the net usable floor space. Thus the corridor would border all four sides of the core. All remaining space extending from the four sides of the rectangle formed by the corridor to the exterior building walls would be net assignable office space. (See Illustration 7-1.)

In buildings which do not have a square or rectangular pattern or which do not have a service core, the general corridor established as the first artery of the semipublic traffic-circulation pattern would follow other shapes. In an L-shaped building, with elevators and service facilities located at the end of one wing, the general corridor might very well be a

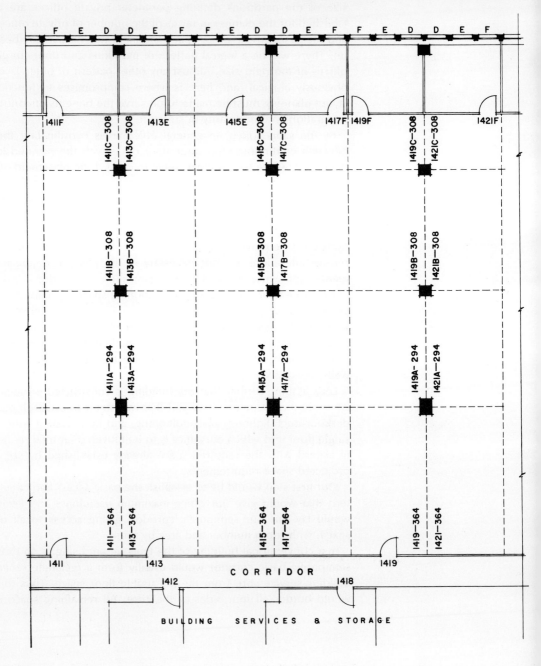

Illus. 7-1. Room numbering and bay area plan of a typical section from the building core to the window wall.

central route extending from the elevators down the length of one wing, then turning in either direction at right angles to divide the second wing.

The first general corridor established may take various forms as long as it satisfies the basic condition for the main corridor in the over-all circulation pattern; that is, it must make every unit of net usable space accessible from the corridor, and thus from every other unit of usable space on the floor. It is this corridor that carries the office worker from work area to elevators, stairwells, washrooms, etc., as well as providing for visitor traffic.

With the first general corridor established in the circulation pattern, the next step the space administrator takes is to assign room numbers to his units of net usable space. The term "room numbers" here does not refer to private office areas: the numbers designate units of space, or space modules, and serve as a first control on assignment and administration of space as well as office space identification. They serve as a final control as well; throughout the life of the building, these units will be identified by the numbers assigned.

We have stipulated that our hypothetical building is constructed on 20- by 20-foot bays. Thus we take as our logical unit of space the structural module itself, the 400 square feet encompassed between each four columns.

In our primary assignment of room numbers, each line of structural modules extending from exterior wall to corridor is numbered. Numbers are staggered and in sequence in the case of a corridor dividing usable space; thus all bay areas on the right side of the corridor might be designated by odd numbers in sequence, and all the bay areas on the left side of the corridor by even numbers in sequence. (See Illustration 7-1.)

This is the primary space-assignment breakdown by room numbers. Now we have our entire usable floor area "sliced" into a basic space pattern, with each slice of usable area designated by number. We may, however, have several of our basic structural modules, the 20- by 20-foot bay, in each slice of space extending from the 20-foot span between columns at the exterior wall to the corridor. We designate each of these modules by letter. Thus, reading from the corridor to the exterior wall, our final room-number designation might be for one given line 4 modules deep:

1417, 1417a, 1417b, 1417c

The 14 would of course refer to the floor. Room 1417 would be the first 20- by 20-foot module directly off the corridor, 1417a the next in the line from corridor to the exterior wall, 1417b the next, and 1417c the module at the building's exterior wall.

Once room numbers are established, so that all subsequent plans can be worked out on a basis of exact assignment to specific numbered areas, each such area can also have area in square feet indicated. Thus we can use the room number and area references in tabulating and exercising space control.

At this point we begin to work out our internal interdepartmental circulation pattern. In the hypothetical building we have been considering, our column span is 20 feet, and we plan to put our private offices on the perimeter of the building. Thus we have established almost automatically our exterior interdepartmental corridors separating outer private offices from inner general offices.

All we have to do, remembering that the corridor can be placed between the first interior line of columns, and the window wall, or on the interior side of the first line of columns, is check our recommended space standards for private offices—economical or liberal—to see what depth we want to use. Placing the corridor on the interior side of the columns will make each private office 20 feet deep; placing it between columns and exterior wall will decrease the depth of each private office by the width of the corridor.

If we have set a square-foot standard demanding offices 20 feet deep for executive positions and, say, 15 feet deep for administrative positions, location of our first exterior interdepartmental corridors is established for us.

The corridor separating executive offices from general office areas will be placed outside the first line of columns; the corridor separating administrative offices from general office areas will be placed between columns and exterior window wall and will be 5 feet wide. If 10 feet it would provide space for secretaries and assistants.

If executive and administrative offices occur in the same row, a straight corridor can still be provided by placing the corridor inside the first line of columns and then grouping all executive offices together and all administrative offices together. The 5 feet of free space between the partitions fronting the administrative offices and the corridor can be used to house secretaries and assistants serving the administrative offices. If we use columnless office space, we would then be guided by the ceiling modules. A 5-foot ceiling module would provide a liberal standard, and a 4-foot module an economical standard.

Now we have established the depth of all private offices and interdepartmental corridors running completely around our office space, assuming that the entire perimeter of the floor is occupied by private offices. Some layouts may dictate reversing the general practice of placing private offices on the perimeter of the floor; the more efficient layout may dictate placing general office areas at the windows, private offices in the interior. (See Illustration 7-2.) The remaining or usable space can now be devoted to the one best layout for departmental general office space and special areas. Our over-all departmental groupings will in turn suggest a logical pattern for smaller corridors and crossover aisles within the general office areas.

By setting up our main circulation patterns, we have already suggested

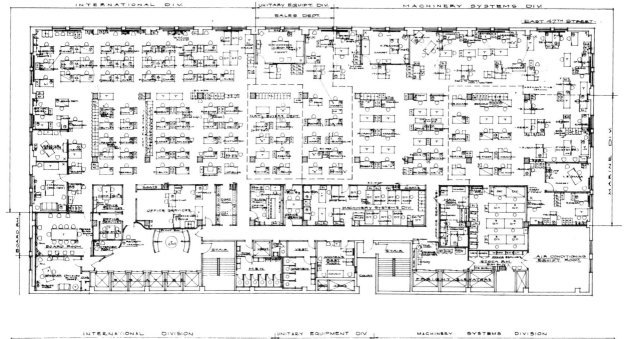

Illus. 7-2. Interior offices versus exterior offices.
(*Courtesy of Carrier Air Conditioning Corp.*)

Illus. 7-2 (Cont.) Exterior view.

the locations for our main air-conditioning ducts. Now we can plan for our general office area's underfloor ducts, which will run parallel to the building wall down the long dimension of the office, and our ceiling lighting, which will run at right angles to the building wall, across the short dimension of the office or in a modular non-directional pattern.

The lighting layout is sometimes altered in engineering, architectural, or drafting rooms where it is most desirable to have the lighting fixtures run parallel to the drawing-board lanes, even though this may require placement of light strips parallel to building walls. Such departments must have shadowless lighting and so must always have direct overhead illumination. This means that drafting tables must be placed directly underneath the lighting strips at right angles to the strips, and lighting provided in non-directional modularity for complete flexibility of layout.

Assuming we have set up our space standards for individual workers at the median figure of 80 square feet, it is almost imperative that we lay our parallel underfloor electric and telephone ducts at intervals of 5 feet. Wider intervals between the ducts will almost force a more generous space allotment per worker if the desks are to be spaced individually. Once underfloor ducts have been put in, the office-space layout planning standards are frozen, since a major reconstruction job is required to install a new underfloor-duct pattern. Thus even if a more generous space allotment is decided on, it is wise to use a 4- or 5-foot interval when space is first being reconditioned or built, since this allows practically any reasonable space standard to be used in general office areas in the future. Intervals of 8 or 10 feet between ducts limit the desk pattern too much and force the space administrator to tailor his layout to his underfloor-duct patterns at all times to a liberal space allotment standard.

If continuous-strip lighting or glowing ceilings are used, we have found it best to place the lighting strips on 10-foot centers—in other words, with 10-foot intervals between each row of lights if 20 by 20 is the structural module. Placement of the lighting strips is made 5 feet from the building column for the best lighting pattern. Thus in each 20 by 20-foot bay, there would be two lighting strips inset 5 feet from the columns that define the bay. If a modular ceiling is used, it might affect the 20-foot dimension.

Air-conditioning ducts are also placed on 10-foot centers in the 20 by 20-foot bay pattern with two supply grills for each bay (see Illustration 7-3). This concept has been used a lot in investor-speculative-type buildings.

For total modularity in ceiling design, see Illustration 7-4.

All these architectural and engineering techniques for the control of space presuppose that management, in the move to new space, will set as its objectives the best air-conditioning arrangements, the best lighting, and the best underfloor-duct pattern to create a truly contemporary office.

How much of an adaptation job does this involve in conditioning existing space in a building constructed, say, forty to fifty years ago?

It may sound overwhelming. Actually, it's not too formidable. As a

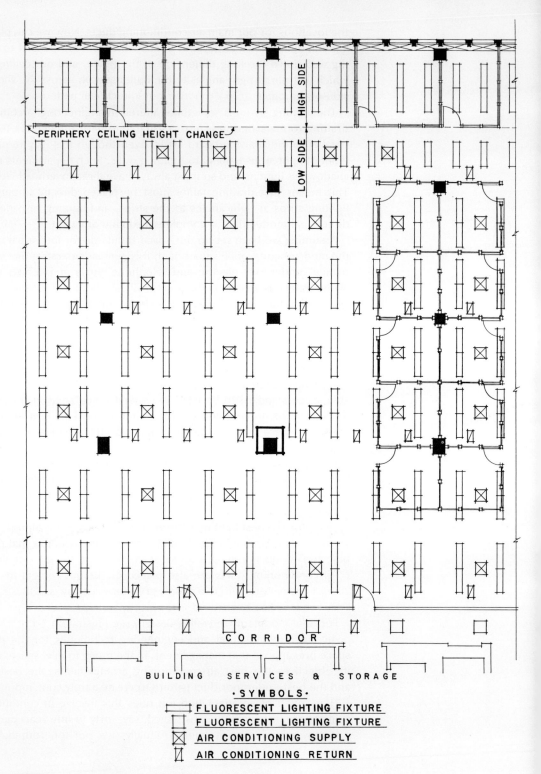

PERIPHERY CEILING HEIGHT CHANGE

HIGH SIDE

LOW SIDE

C O R R I D O R

B U I L D I N G   S E R V I C E S   &   S T O R A G E

·SYMBOLS·

FLUORESCENT LIGHTING FIXTURE
FLUORESCENT LIGHTING FIXTURE
AIR CONDITIONING SUPPLY
AIR CONDITIONING RETURN

Illus. 7-3. Air-conditioning and electric lighting layout.

matter of fact, very often a company is better advised to modernize existing space in an old building than to rent space in a brand new building, even when new buildings are under construction and so can be adapted to incorporate features specified by the tenant or owner.

Let's see just what *is* involved in installing air conditioning, hung ceilings, underfloor ducts, and all the other physical and mechanical building elements discussed in this chapter.

AIR CONDITIONING

Air conditioning, considered questionable on many grounds just a few years ago, is a required standard for today's office. Certainly it would be a rare office that would plan on moving into new space without providing for maintenance of a healthful working temperature the year round.

Actually air conditioning is more than just temperature control. In spite of the emphasis on air conditioning as a cooling agent—which is certainly important in hot American summers—the fact is that a good air-conditioning system circulates properly tempered, humidified, and filtered air throughout the office all year round.

In addition to providing air cleanliness, adequate ventilation, control of temperature and relative humidity, and elimination of drafts through proper supply and distribution systems, air-conditioning an office also serves to eliminate outside noise and dust, since windows are kept closed at all times.

In large office buildings we generally advocate a system that gives the best possible control of temperature at the window areas of the building without creating drafts in the interior general office space. This is accomplished by using window units or periphery linear ceiling air supply ducts which air-condition an area extending in depth 15 to 25 feet in from the building wall.

Thus, in the general arrangement under which private offices are placed around the perimeter of the building, these offices, which are subject to rapid temperature changes, are air-conditioned by window or ceiling units either automatically or manually controlled. The interdepartmental corridor separating perimeter private offices from interior general office space usually has a hung ceiling covering a main supply and a return duct. A plenum-chamber arrangement might then be used for conditioning the interior office space, a hung ceiling of perforated material covering the entire interior area. The ducts above the corridor pour cooled air, through finger ducts, into the space between hung ceilings and true ceilings. The cooled air then filters down, like gentle rain, through the perforations of the hung ceiling to the general office areas.

When a plenum-chamber air distribution system is not possible in an office, the conventional duct supply and return system is used. Under the conventional system, the fresh air blowing through the ducts above the corridor is blown out through branch ducts and supply grills in each bay or part

Illus. 7-4. Luminglas Glowing Ceiling design combining air conditioning, lighting, and sound conditioning. (a) Plan; (b) section through general office; (c) section through private office and general office.

of a modular patterned suspension system. Return ducts are in wall or ceiling outlets located in the general office or in specified corridor locations.

Illustration 7-4 shows a typical example of such an air-conditioning layout. Note that in the outer or perimeter offices air is supplied through side wall grills or individual air-conditioning units are placed at the window sill. The general office area is cooled by a plenum chamber, with a perforated hung ceiling to diffuse the air.

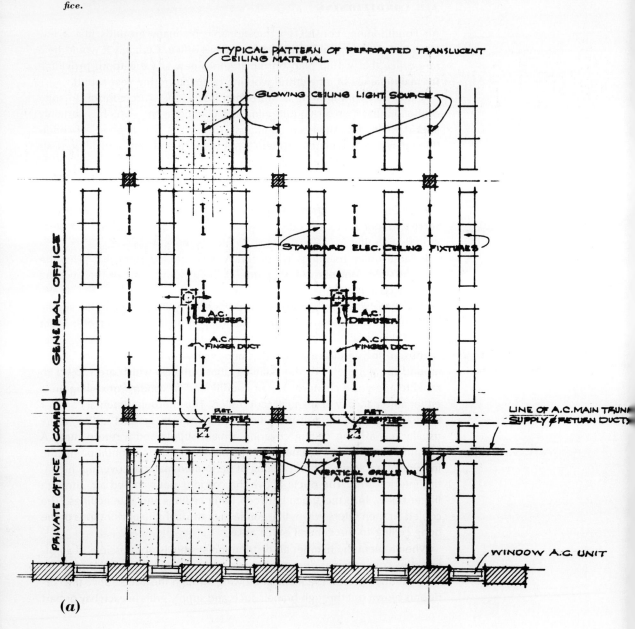

(a)

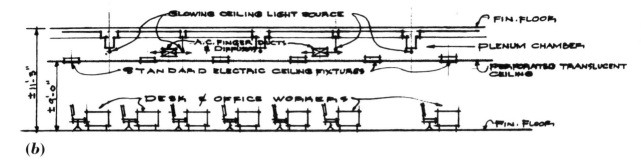

(b)

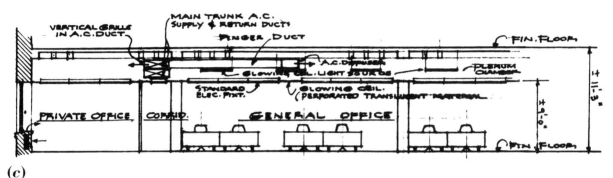

(c)

The American Society of Heating and Ventilating Engineers recommends for office buildings a temperature range of from 74 to 78°F summer and winter and a relative humidity of 40 to 50 per cent in the summer and 30 to 40 per cent in the winter.

At this point I would like to quote from an article in *Skyscraper Management,* official publication of Building Owners and Managers Association, by A. A. Giannini of Carrier Air Conditioning Corporation, whose system of air conditioning was used in the United States Steel Building, Pittsburgh, Pennsylvania.

> Outstanding progress has been made since the systems used in office buildings were mainly adaptations of low-pressure systems that were developed for large open spaces. Not until the 1940's was a system developed expressly for multi-story office buildings.
>
> The high-pressure conduit system rapidly became, and still is, the most widely used system for the perimeter areas of office buildings. (See Illustration 7-5.)
>
> Perimeter Zone: Coincident with the introduction of the conduit system was the concept of separating, for air conditioning design purposes, the perimeter portion of a building from its interior. The perimeter zone extended 12 to 20 feet into the building, thereby including the private offices that were then being placed along exterior walls.
>
> The reason for "zoning" a building is that the effect of sunlight and the difference between indoor and outdoor temperatures is felt primarily at or near the building's skin. If the perimeter is handled by a separate system that will account for transmission effects, thereby acting as a buffer zone, then the interior spaces will have a relatively light and stable heat load derived from only lighting fixtures, office machines and people. In fact, interior zones need cooling throughout the

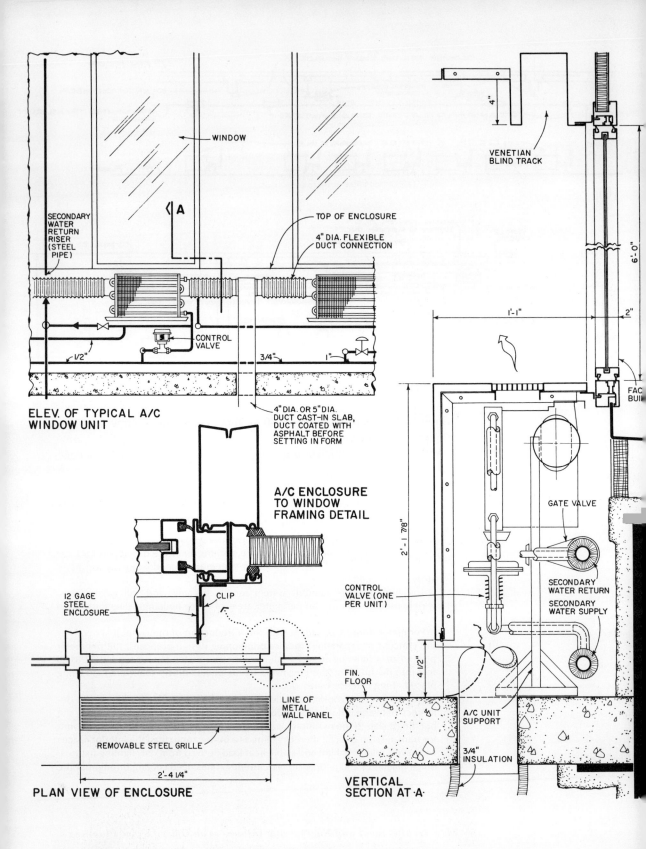

WINDOW

A

SECONDARY
WATER
RETURN
RISER
(STEEL
PIPE)

TOP OF ENCLOSURE

4" DIA. FLEXIBLE
DUCT CONNECTION

CONTROL
VALVE

1/2"

3/4"

1"

4" DIA. OR 5" DIA.
DUCT CAST-IN SLAB,
DUCT COATED WITH
ASPHALT BEFORE
SETTING IN FORM

**ELEV. OF TYPICAL A/C
WINDOW UNIT**

**A/C ENCLOSURE
TO WINDOW
FRAMING DETAIL**

12 GAGE
STEEL
ENCLOSURE

CLIP

LINE OF
METAL
WALL PANEL

REMOVABLE STEEL GRILLE

2'-4 1/4"

PLAN VIEW OF ENCLOSURE

VENETIAN
BLIND TRACK

4"

6'-0"

1'-1"

2"

FAC
BUI

GATE VALVE

CONTROL
VALVE (ONE
PER UNIT)

SECONDARY
WATER RETURN

SECONDARY
WATER SUPPLY

2'-1 7/8"

4 1/2"

FIN.
FLOOR

A/C UNIT
SUPPORT

3/4"
INSULATION

**VERTICAL
SECTION AT ·A·**

year while perimeter areas may require simultaneous heating and cooling along different wall exposures, particularly for in-between seasons.

Interior-zone system: In recent years, however a need for individual temperature control in interior spaces has become necessary because of the increase and variance in lighting levels, the trend toward the placement of private offices and conference rooms in the interior, and the constantly changing requirements for interior space as building occupancy changes. But until the last few years there has not been a system for interior zones that could match the excellence of control flexibility of perimeter zone systems, at least not at reasonable cost and space requirements.

In addition to providing individual temperature control in a variety of spaces, a quality interior-zone air conditioning system should be of such design that the system can be installed before final office layout needs are known. This makes it possible to contract for a completed building without adding the "moving in" costs for altering the system to account for last-minute partition changes. And the system should provide this flexibility throughout the building's life, requiring no major alterations regardless of tenant requirements. That is why the module of 4' or 5' or whatever is so important during the design stage.

One system that offers both individual temperature control and total flexibility in office arrangement is the Dual Moduline system. It is installed in the new United States Steel Headquarters Building in Pittsburgh. (See Illustration 7-6a.)

Dual Moduline System: Instead of providing a constant quantity of air and varying its temperature to meet changing interior loads, typical to dual duct, the Dual Moduline system supplies variable quantities of cool air at a constant temperature. Heart of the system is an automatic throttling device that maintains high air discharge velocities to prevent drafts and reduce outlet noise as was common with early variable volume systems.

The system's diffuser sections or terminal units are recessed in the ceiling, and can be installed in any type of hung ceiling. All is delivered through two long, narrow slots tangent to the ceiling, creating a negative pressure above the air stream that causes the stream to hug the ceiling. This is the Bernoulli principle of aerodynamics, which gives an airplane wing its lift.

The only visible portion of the terminal is a 3-inch-wide diffuser with an outlet slot on each side and a flat blank space between that will permit the installation of a standard partition or "wall panel" directly beneath the unit. When serving an open space, the terminal may be equipped with a single control that can serve up to four slave units. When installed over a partition, the terminal is equipped with dual controls to provide varying air quantities out of each slot and therefore give individual temperature control in each space. (See Illustration 7-6c.)

The controls are powered by the conditioned air itself, and automatically adjust air flow to compensate for varying temperature loads. As lights are turned

(a)

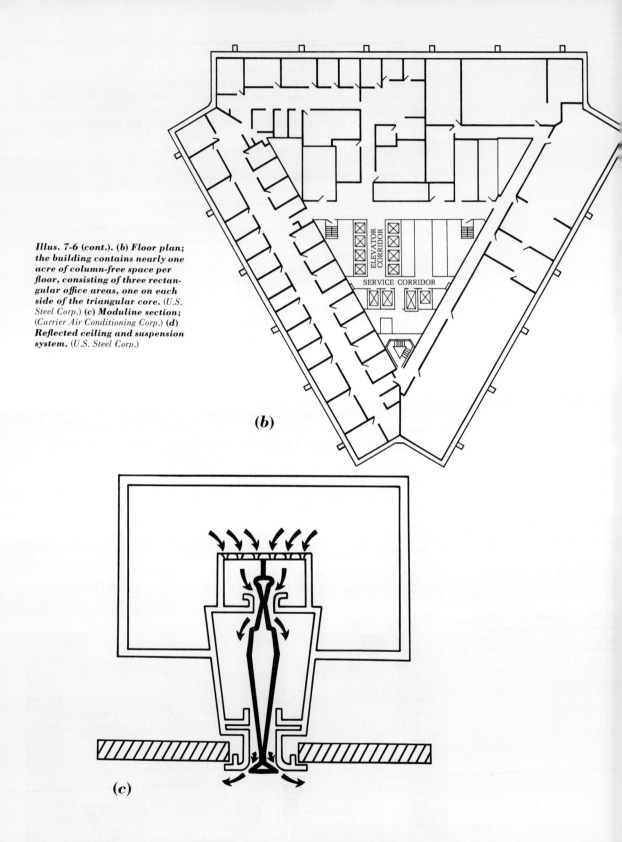

Illus. 7-6 (cont.). (b) Floor plan; the building contains nearly one acre of column-free space per floor, consisting of three rectangular office areas, one on each side of the triangular core. (U.S. Steel Corp.) (c) Moduline section; (Carrier Air Conditioning Corp.) (d) Reflected ceiling and suspension system. (U.S. Steel Corp.)

ELEVATOR CORRIDOR

SERVICE CORRIDOR

(b)

(c)

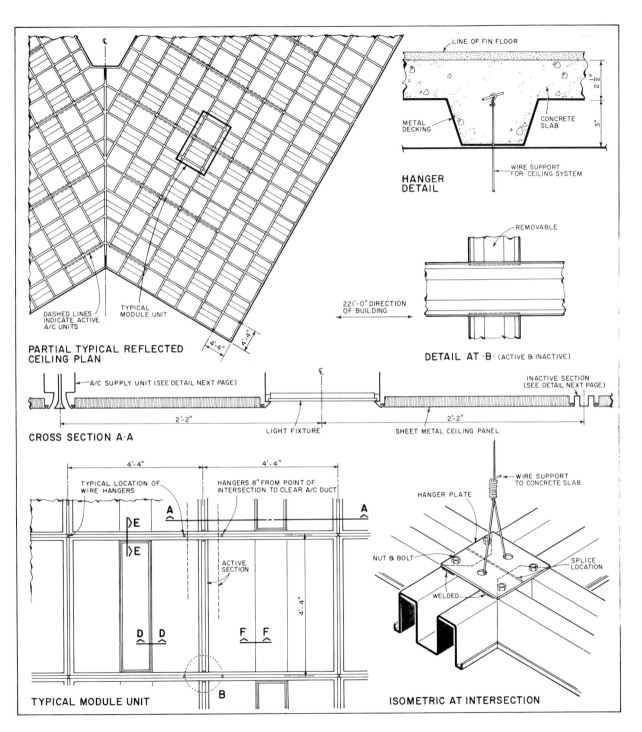

LINE OF FIN. FLOOR

METAL DECKING

CONCRETE SLAB

$2\frac{1}{2}''$

3"

WIRE SUPPORT FOR CEILING SYSTEM

HANGER DETAIL

REMOVABLE

221'-0" DIRECTION OF BUILDING

DETAIL AT ·B· (ACTIVE & INACTIVE)

DASHED LINES INDICATE ACTIVE A/C UNITS

TYPICAL MODULE UNIT

4'-4"

4'-4"

PARTIAL TYPICAL REFLECTED CEILING PLAN

A/C SUPPLY UNIT (SEE DETAIL NEXT PAGE)

INACTIVE SECTION (SEE DETAIL NEXT PAGE)

2'-2"

LIGHT FIXTURE

SHEET METAL CEILING PANEL

2'-2"

CROSS SECTION A·A

4'-4"

4'-4"

TYPICAL LOCATION OF WIRE HANGERS

HANGERS 8" FROM POINT OF INTERSECTION TO CLEAR A/C DUCT

A   A

E

E

ACTIVE SECTION

4'-4"

D D

F F

B

TYPICAL MODULE UNIT

WIRE SUPPORT TO CONCRETE SLAB

HANGER PLATE

NUT & BOLT

SPLICE LOCATION

WELDED

ISOMETRIC AT INTERSECTION

(d) *(See following page for enlarged details of cross section A-A.)*

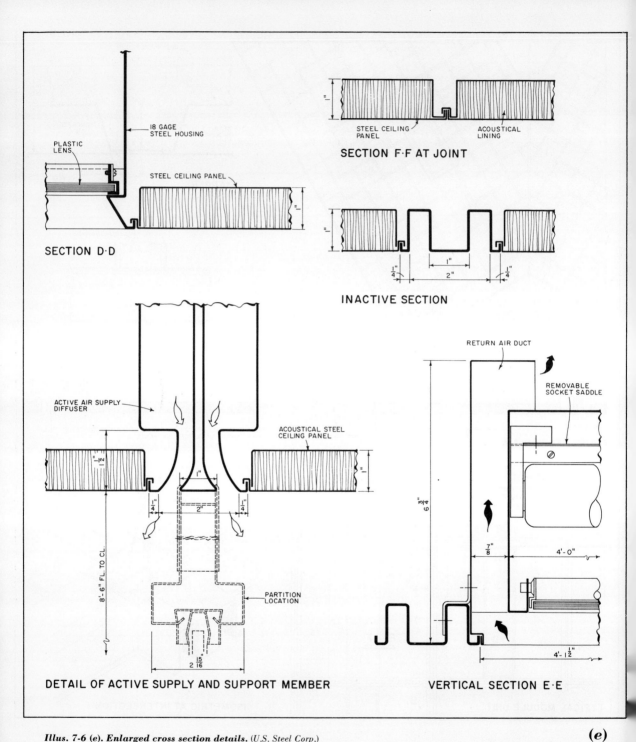

Illus. 7-6 (e). Enlarged cross section details. (U.S. Steel Corp.)

off and people leave a space, air flow to that space is automatically reduced. In effect, the system follows moving heat loads.

The modular concept of the Dual Moduline, coupled with totally automatic control, makes it possible to erect partitions in any arrangement without changing the air conditioning outlets or ductwork, and without the difficult "rebalancing" required with conventional systems. Controls are simply slipped in or out of the terminals as required to serve open spaces or adjoining offices.

The diffusers become an integral part of the ceiling structure, with the linear diffuser located along grid lines in conformity with the dimensions chosen for the modules, normally the 4' or 5' dimension. Return air is through the plenum, placing grilles in the ceiling panels as required, or slots matching the supply air diffuser.

Use of Lighting Fixtures: With air conditioning supply located through channel strips, this location leaves the center of each 4' or 5' free for location of lighting fixtures, acoustical panels, and return air grilles, thereby separating the three unrelated functions of air conditioning, sound conditioning, and lighting, and permitting the use of any type of lighting and acoustical material.

Prefabrication and systems building are most important to the owner, architect, and builder today.

LIGHTING

Office lighting today has revolutionized the entire office scene. In today's office, the wall and ceiling colors, as well as the floor and office equipment, are all coordinated with the desired lighting intensities. Dark walls, floors, and furniture are out of harmony with 75 to 150 foot-candles of lighting. (See Illustration 7-7.)

The Illuminating Engineering Society makes several recommendations regarding lighting intensities. In the Fifth Edition, March, 1972, the following lighting recommendations were approved for office areas:

Illus. 7-7. Recommended surface reflectances for offices. (*Courtesy of Illuminating Engineering Society.*)

Type of Work	Currently Recommended Illumination, foot-candles
Cartography, designing, and detailed drafting	200
Accounting, auditing, tabulating, bookkeeping, business machine operation, reading poor reproductions, rough layout drafting	150
Regular office work, reading good reproductions, reading or transcribing handwriting in hard pencil or on poor paper, active filing, index references, mail sorting	100
Reading or transcribing handwriting in ink or medium pencil on good-quality paper, intermittent filing	70
Reading high-contrast or well-printed material; tasks not involving critical or prolonged seeing, such as conferring and interviewing; areas such as inactive files and washrooms	30
Corridors, elevators, escalators, stairways	20
For eye comfort, not less than one-third to one-fifth in adjacent areas.	

In general office areas, it is advisable to have at least 100 to 150 maintained foot-candles of light in all areas. (Maintained value is what can be expected after six months of operation. Naturally, dust on fixtures and loss of original brightness of fluorescent tubes depreciate the initial light output, sometimes as much as 20 per cent.) Private offices may not require such high general illumination. Approximately 40 to 50 maintained foot-candles is enough for general lighting, but supplementary lighting is then required directly over the work area. Specialized clerical workers, such as accounting department personnel, who must handle detailed figures on papers with little color contrast, may require as much as 200 foot-candles throughout their work areas, as may personnel in engineering and drafting rooms.

Lavatories, building-service areas, and corridors can be adequately lighted by 30 to 40 foot-candles.

There are many ways of attaining the recommended lighting levels for office areas, but perhaps the most effective is through use of 2-foot-wide by 4-foot-long fixtures in parallel strips spaced 10 feet apart in private and general office areas. These are used where the ceiling height is between 9 and 10 feet. The fixtures are controlled locally by column switches or by a master board. For special work, a pendant fixture may be used instead of a unit set flush in the ceiling or recessed.

The differing light levels specified for different types of work may be maintained with uniform fixtures since a varying number of tubes may be used within each fixture. The 2-foot-wide fixture recommended can be used with as few as two 4-foot fluorescent tubes or as many as six, depending on the desired lighting intensity.

The luminous ceiling, in which translucent plastic or glass covers the entire ceiling, has been used in highly stylized offices of late, but monotony of appearance, high installation and maintenance costs, and high heat load affecting the air-conditioning operating costs are major disadvantages.

The Luminglas Glowing Ceiling shown in Illustration 7-4 has all the advantages of the luminous ceiling and overcomes its several disadvantages, plus supplying air conditioning and sound control. There is no need for the great number of fluorescent tubes above the ceiling to provide office lighting, as desired lighting intensities are supplied by the conventional office-lighting fixtures located as shown in the illustration. Original electric installation and maintenance costs of office lighting are reduced, as there is only one fluorescent tube for every 100 square feet in the plenum-chamber space. This one tube is used to give a luminous effect to the perforated plastic. The plenum chamber satisfies air-conditioning distribution, and the fluorescent tubes used to give the glowing effect do not increase the heat load enough to affect air-conditioning operating costs, as in the luminous ceiling.

It is believed lighting, air conditioning, and sound conditioning in the office of the future will employ many imaginative designs in modular ceiling combinations.

UNDERFLOOR DUCTS

In older buildings, it is usually relatively simple to install underfloor ducts, because conventional construction a generation ago employed cement topping over cinder fill above the floor slab. Thus there is adequate space to install ducts by cutting and installing the duct between the cement topping and the structural slab.

In new buildings, the underfloor-duct system is likewise laid in the fill. The underfloor-duct system shown in Illustration 7-8, or some similar system, is one of the better types because it allows for three lines—a high-tension line, a low-tension line, and an intercom and buzzer-system line. Still another duct plan is embodied in the corrugated-deck floor arrangement which acts as a structural unit, and, because of its cellular shape, can also carry various high-and low-tension lines as well as air ducts (see Illustration 7-9).

Illus. 7-8. Typical underfloor duct in conventional concrete floor construction. (*Walker-Parkersburg.*)

Many buildings are being constructed without underfloor systems for electric, telephone, and low-tension wiring; instead, wires are run within the plenum space of hung ceilings and supply services to the floors above through holes punched into those floors. Other systems use the plenum space for getting to required electric and telephone locations through the Tele-Power poles (see Illustration 7-10) and Elephant trunklines (see Illustration 7-11).

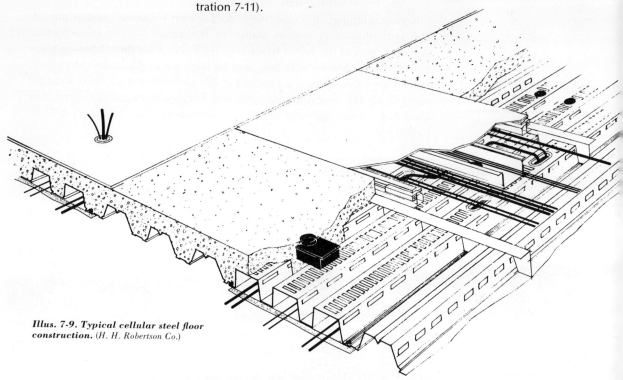

Illus. 7-9. Typical cellular steel floor construction. (H. H. Robertson Co.)

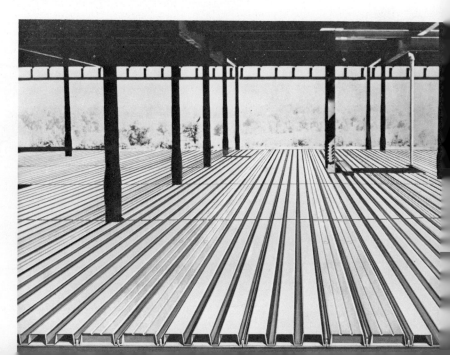

Illus. 7-10. Tele-Power poles.
(*Wiremold Company.*)

Illus. 7-11. Elephant trunklines.

COLUMN SPANS AND
CEILING HEIGHTS

Steel beam and girder spans of about 20 to 40 feet in each direction provide a good working module well suited to layout planning for the average company's private offices, general offices, and special-purpose areas. For the largest companies, it has been found that the optimum economical column center is about 35 feet for general office areas. Even in very large companies, it has been found that the desk clusters seldom exceed 35 feet in width, even though we hear of 60-foot-wide columnless office space. Ceiling heights in an office may vary considerably through use of hung ceilings beneath the true ceiling. In the average situation, we have found that having ceilings in corridors about 8 feet high, in private offices 9 feet high, and in general offices 10 to 15 feet high is good practice. Where panelwall dividers are used from floor to ceiling, it is suggested ceilings range from 8½ to 12½ feet in height.

Varying ceiling heights in different areas of the office, besides relieving visual monotony, make it possible to hide duct work for the air conditioning, help solve unusual lighting and acoustical problems, and help control and influence the use of space.

Ceiling construction may be wire lath and plaster or other materials. Various perforated materials, such as metal or plastic, may be used with or without a concealed air-conditioning system and built-in lighting fixtures. Sometimes, too, egg-crate or similar ceiling construction may be used to advantage, although cleaning and maintenance problems may be increased. A luminous glowing ceiling made of translucent corrugated plastic or glass, with light sources concealed above the plastic or glass, can be extremely effective in combination with conventional lighting fixtures. As mentioned, this type of ceiling can also be ordered in a perforated version where a plenum-chamber air-conditioning system is used to distribute cooled draftless air down through the ceiling.

ACOUSTICS

Today's office demands acoustical treatment. This is a must, not only in terms of making the office a more pleasant place to work, but also as a means of keeping employee efficiency high. The methods and materials used to keep the office sound level low, however, may vary widely. One very effective system is the use of a perforated metal or composition-pan hung ceiling with sound-absorbing material above it. Flat or angular sound panels may be incorporated in the design of a modular ceiling, as shown in Illustration 7-6. Special sound-absorbing materials resembling plaster may be used for the finish on both walls and ceilings. Still another method employs special composition-tile materials which are cemented directly to the true ceiling surfaces or framed in mechanical suspension systems.

Floor and wall carpeting, drapes and curtains, and upholstered furniture, are sound absorbing surfaces which help eliminate office noises.

There is a wide range of alternatives in sound-conditioning the office, and analysis will lead to the best solution for any specific office. Regardless of the method or material used, however, the value of keeping the office noise level fairly low is well established as a desirable psychological and physiological factor.

ENERGY CONSERVATION*

The need for energy conservation is a major concern of office administrators. Thirty-four per cent of the total national consumption of energy is used in heating, cooling, and lighting of commercial and residential structures as compared with 41 per cent for industrial usage and 25 per cent for transportation. Recent directives by GSA have established a 7 per cent energy savings goal in federal office installations in 1973. An obvious method of obtaining such savings is the traditional cry of "turn off the lights." This method not only saves the initial lighting energy but also the energy required to cool the heated air produced by the lighting fixtures.

Other less primative methods should be reviewed in both existing facilities and during the design phases of new installations.

1. *Insulation:* Increased costs for improved insulation will provide trade-offs in reduction of mechanical installation and long-term operating costs.

2. *Glazing:* Load reduction can be obtained from special reflective and heat-absorbing glasses as well as from double glazing of windows. Shading should be considered as well as the effects of the number of windows on the exterior wall and the ability to control and use natural lighting.

3. *Lighting:* Serious consideration of the basic assumptions under which one is operating can result in significant savings. Must you have 100 foot-candles of general illumination at all times? Lighting heat loads now make up 50 per cent of the total cooling requirements of the average office space. Are lower levels, task lighting, and natural light suitable to your needs? The decision to use fluorescent rather than incandescent fixtures represents an energy savings of three to five times for equivalent lighting. Use of lighter colors should be considered.

4. *HVAC:* Do we need what we now have? The increase of heating levels above 70°F can cost 3 per cent more for each degree farenheit, while setting back the night thermostat can save 1 to 1.5 per cent per degree farenheit. Humidity levels can be dropped at the end of the day, ventilation air changes can be reduced, and heat-recovery devices can be installed. Total energy systems, in which waste heat from electrical generation is captured for space heating and in which solar energy is utilized, are becoming practical methods of installation which merit serious attention.

5. *Operations:* A well-maintained system can increase efficiency 10 per cent with an equivalent energy savings. Selective operation of portions of the system and isolation of heat producing equipment offer savings to a continuous management overview of systems operation and a specific energy conservation program.

* In collorboration with Haines, Lundberg, & Waehler: Architectural Engineers.

eight

PLANNING OFFICE SERVICES
AND BUILDING SERVICES

OFFICE SERVICES

E very office requires basic office services, and location and functional layout for the areas housing these services must be carefully planned. In the small organization, the basic service areas will be relatively few and may even be physically located within the general office. But as we go up the scale of company size, service areas become more numerous and more complex until, in a giant corporation, they occupy a large proportion of office space. The basic similarity between a very small office and a very large one is underlined, however, by the fact that in each certain services must be established and by the fact that in every office layout there is one best place for each major service, in terms of the departments making greatest use of it and its accessibility and adjacency.

Typical office service areas are mail rooms, conference rooms, duplicating, storage, reception rooms, central transcription, word processing, filing departments, transfer-filing, telephone and teletype centers and the many duplicating machines. In larger corporations, machine-tabulating rooms, or even electronic data-processing centers, may be added to the list. A central business library is a necessity in many companies.

What might be termed "employees' service areas" must also be planned in the modern office. These include such necessities as coat rooms and in today's larger offices embrace a whole range of other facilities as well: dispensary, employees' lounge, cafeteria or snack bar, employees' library. An extremely large office would probably plan other employee facilities in addition to lounges and library, such as an auditorium (which can also be used as a theater), game room, bowling alleys, perhaps even a gymnasium and health club. Some suburban offices have even included barber shops, beauty parlors, and small stores selling general merchandise or company products in their office space.

A service area necessary to nearly every company is a reception room of some kind, which may also be used for exhibits of company products. Increasingly common is a communications center, used both to pipe music through the office areas and to send announcements over the public address system. And very large companies may find it useful to have a machine-repair room for maintenance and storage of office equipment, as well as storage space for office furniture, screens, and panelwalls, today.

And—not to be overlooked—such small but essential things as water coolers, exit signs, clocks, bulletin boards, and time clocks must also be placed throughout the office in the particular spots where they will serve the greatest number of people most efficiently.

Let's analyze each of these facilities and services in terms of its specific requirements and its place in the over-all layout scheme.

Mail Rooms

The size and location of the company mail room are directly controlled by the size of the corporation which it serves. In a very small company, occupying comparatively little space, location of the mail room is not too important a factor, since it cannot possibly be too far away from any of the departments it serves. A "mail room" in an extremely small office may be a set of postal scales and a postage meter located on a table next to a secretary's desk. She will assume, in addition to her other responsibilities, the duty of seeing that the mail is properly weighed and stamped each day. The office boy will probably distribute the incoming mail. Here the mailroom location is determined by the location of the person responsible for seeing that the mail gets out. Whatever is the one best place for that person in the performance of her major duties becomes the one best place for the mailing equipment. This is the type of mail room generally found in offices with less than thirty personnel.

At the other end of the scale is the large corporation where mailroom activities demand a full-time supervisor with a corps of employees and mail movement may require an elaborate mechanical system involving distribution to and collection from substations throughout the building. Often movement of mail and interoffice papers is speeded from one station to another by a system of pneumatic tubes or conveyers serving all parts of the building.

At this extreme, the best location of the mail room is determined by two factors: it should be located at some point easily reached from the outside, and it should also have quick access to all departments of the company. Usually in a large installation the mail room will be on the ground floor of the building, if the company occupies its own structure, or on the lowest floor of rented quarters. This makes the handling of bulky mail bags as simple as possible. By the same token, it should be convenient to elevators. Obviously, however, if dumb-waiters or pneumatic-tube delivery and collection systems are used, the mechanical requirements controlling the installation of such carriers will control to a large degree the exact location of the mail room.

In companies which fall between the two extremes cited—companies which do have a true mail room, staffed by full-time employees, but which deliver and collect mail through ordinary manual pick-up—placement of the department in relation to its volume of traffic with other departments should be the determining factor. Teletype, filing, central stenographic, shipping, duplicating, and loading departments are, each in its way, naturally complementary to the mailing department. The word processing needs of a particular company should decide which of these departments should be given most weight in planning the location of the mail department.

In determining the space to be allotted to the mail department, the work load and the machines which must be used to carry that load should be the major factors considered. The extent to which letter-opening machines are used, the amount of table space needed for sorting racks, scales, and postage meters, the number of small carts or carriages needed to distribute mail, and the number of mail sacks to be housed are facts that must be known. Obviously, too, the planner must know the number of people who will work in the department. (Illustrations 8-1 and 8-2 show a typical small mail-room layout and a large mail room.)

Illus. 8-1. Small mail room layout. Even in a mail room of limited size, the flow of incoming and outgoing mail is separated to allow uninterrupted movement of mail and personnel. The ability to combine convenient storage space for supplies beneath the work surface of the consoles with maximum sorting capability above the consoles provides efficient utilization of existing floor space. (Pitney Bowes.)

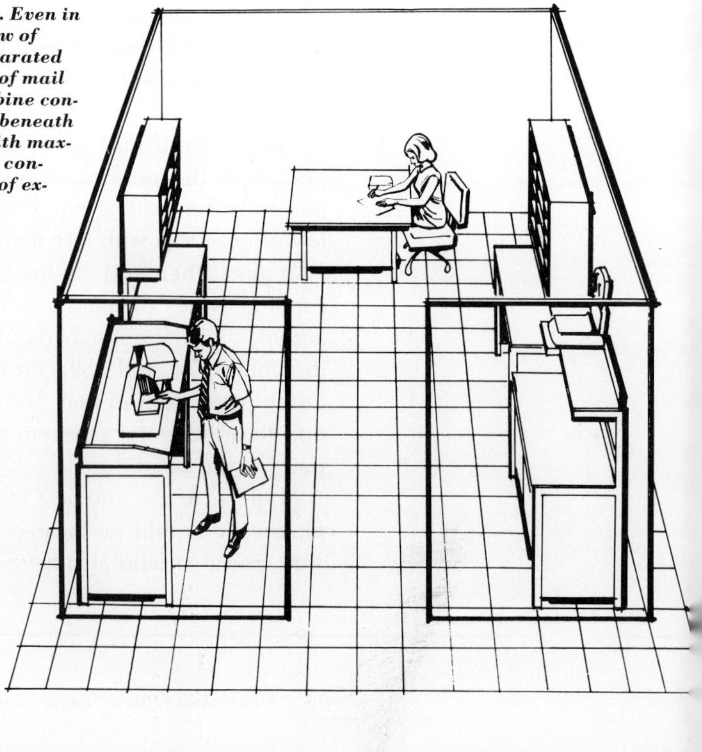

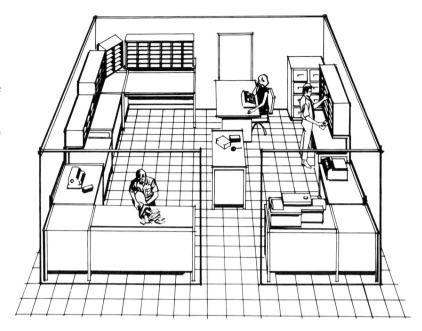

Illus. 8-2. Large mail room layout. The key to efficient mail flow in a mail room with intermediate volume is the preparation of incoming and outgoing patterns for uninterrupted processing. Incoming functions most commonly encountered are dumping, opening, reading, and sorting. Out going functions include separation of mail by class or destination as well as processing via sealing, metering, and bagging. Each function demands a particular type of console to optimize mail handling. Location of each type of console within the incoming and outgoing mail patterns is the common denominator of mail room layout. Processing of the outgoing mail is completed within close proximity to the exit door. Placement of consoles in the incoming section allows the incoming mail to be dumped immediately inside the entrance door. An efficient balance is maintained between people, equipment, and space in providing a total mailing system. (Pitney Bowes.)

Conference Rooms

Conference rooms can be handled in many different ways, depending on the primary purpose for which each room is to be used. Such rooms may have as their main function the housing of work conferences between individual executives representing various departments of the company. They may be placed next to general office areas for meetings between personnel who do not have private offices. Last of all, they may be designed primarily for top-level meetings between officers of the company, top company officials and customers, or for meetings of the board. Obviously, the location and décor of such conference rooms will vary with their major purpose.

After determining the use to which the room is to be put, the space administrator should ensure that the required facilities are built into it. Such facilities might include chalk boards, tack-up boards, motion-picture screen, storage space, or an adjoining room to house motion-picture or slide projectors and sound equipment. In companies which use large conference rooms for auditorium purposes, such as training personnel, a rostrum or platform might be necessary. Large conference rooms or board rooms very often have an attached foyer or lounge with coat-room facilities, telephone, and toilet. Sometimes they have television and a pantry or full kitchen facilities as well.

Sliding doors which can convert one large conference room into two smaller ones are an important innovation which adds to the usefulness and flexibility of such rooms (see Illustrations 8-3 and 8-4 of a typical conference room for use by department heads, a standard conference room adjoining the general office area, and an officers' conference or board room).

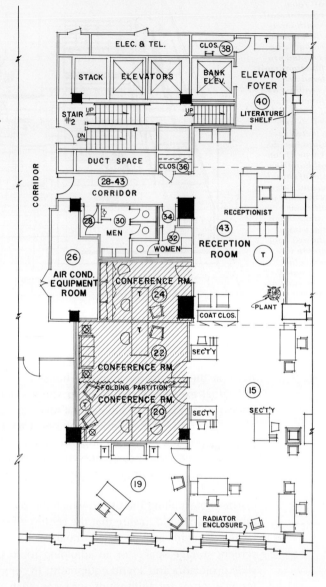

Illus. 8-3. Small conference room or interview office and adjacent flexible conference rooms.

Duplicating Departments

With the rapid spread of paper work, the need to prepare sufficient copies of important reports for all interested executives has increased tremendously the role of the various duplicating processes in the office picture. Today, company duplicating facilities range all the way from the simple gelatin or stencil reproduction machine in the small office to an entire battery of printing and photographic units in the large company, each geared to do certain specific jobs. Since each of these machines, at least in the

Illus. 8-4. Large conference room. (Right) Layout; (Below) photograph.

BOARD ROOM

ASS'T TO PRES.

SHAFT

AIR CONDITIONING ROOM

PANTRY

12

12 A

STOR.

12 C

12 B

STOR.

66 B

FIRE STAIR

RECEPTION

13

66

66 A

17

14

16

18

MEN

58

STOR.

56

60

DRINKING FOUNTAIN

64

FOYER & RECEPTION

54

larger categories, has its own floor-loading, vibration, electric-outlet, and ventilation requirements, detailed programming in terms of the company's present and future needs is necessary in order to give the duplication department the proper location and the proper layout. One thing that should be borne in mind for any duplicating department of any size is, of course, the fact that it should be located close to storage facilities for paper and supplies, if it does not have its own facilities built in.

Storage Facilities

The word "storage" means a variety of things in any discussion of office layout. Storage must be provided for office supplies, record retention, equipment, and maintenance materials. Storage of records and equipment are the least important in terms of location near the active working centers of the office. Record storage, as contrasted with active files, is usually used for records that are referred to occasionally but not as frequently as active files. Since records are usually moved from active to inactive status on a periodic basis and reference to records in inactive storage is comparatively infrequent, accessibility is not a prime factor.

Equipment storage rooms, in our opinion, all too often house equipment which will probably not be used again but which demands constant inventory and protection. Usually a company is much better advised to dispose of surplus equipment as quickly as possible.

Janitorial storage of maintenance materials, although it may not seem important enough to warrant the space consideration at first glance, actually is a serious responsibility. Maintenance is a major office problem and a major office cost. Moreover, paper towels, tissues, bulbs, oils, soaps, and floor-waxing material require active and clean storage. Thus such storage areas should be located as close to the scene where they will be used as possible and, in a large company, should be spotted at various convenient points throughout the office.

The same holds true, of course, for the central office-supply room, which should be located as close as possible to the departments which draw most heavily on the forms, papers, typewriter ribbons, stationery, etc. stocked there. Small supply closets and cabinets, periodically restocked, can be set up in the more remote departments. Of late, "serve yourself" office-supply centers have been established by many companies.

Reception Room

The reception room is the "first appearance" of the company to most visitors, and as such it is important that it be made to express dignity and comfort. A courteous, intelligent attendant or receptionist is, of course, a must. But equally important are physical facilities for the visitors' comfort: enough chairs or settees, ashtrays, coat room or storage space, and, if enough traffic is anticipated, telephone booths and washrooms. Many reception rooms also have visitors' interviewing rooms attached.

Many firms have company exhibits and large replicas of their trade-marks as well as a prominent display of the company's name in the reception area. Interior decoration of the reception room can vary in style all the way from a slightly more elaborate version—in terms of walls, floors, color scheme, and furniture—of the general offices to be found behind the receptionist's desk to highly stylized interiors, utilizing specially built equipment and custom-made furniture in traditional, contemporary, or esoteric design.

Illustrations 8-5 and 8-6 suggest typical treatments for a conventional waiting room and a decorative waiting room.

Illus. 8-5. Conventional reception room.

Central Transcription Department

The replacement of the stenographer—at least as far as departmental executives are concerned—by the nonglamorous but capable dictating machine has given rise in many offices, particularly in larger concerns, to central transcribing pools. There direct dictation from a telephonelike arrangement on the dictator's desk is recorded on tape or record to be transcribed by a pool stenographer. The advantages of such an arrangement, in terms of saving secretarial space in private and general office areas, and also in terms of getting greater stenographic output per worker, are obvious, and so such arrangements are growing more popular every day. Such a transcription department can be located almost anywhere in the office where there is sufficient free space, since its major connection with other departments is a telephonic one. Since the letters it produces, however, must be returned to those who have dictated them for checking and signature the transcription department should be fairly close to the mail-distribution center.

Word Processing

The latest trend in modern office procedures is toward centralized transcription of machine dictation of correspondence and reports. And because of rapidly advancing technology in the equipment which helps perform this task, the nomenclature has changed, as well. The new industry byword describing systemized approaches to handling office paperwork is "word processing," and is defined by IBM (the originator of the concept) as the combination of people, procedures and equipment which transforms ideas into printed communications . . . and helps facilitate the flow of related office work.

The concept is based on the additional productivity available to both authors and secretaries through such devices as remote dictation systems and magnetic media typewriters. The dictation systems enable paperwork originators to record quickly the bulk of their correspondence via telephone or microphone. And, within word processing systems, the dictation is usually channeled directly into the center (or centers) where transcription takes place. There, the typists keyboard their work on such automated typing devices as the IBM Magnetic Tape "Selectric" Typewriter and the IBM Mag Card "Selectric" Typewriter. These machines record typing on a magnetic surface (tape or card). Errors are corrected simply by backspacing and striking over them. When the material has been recorded perfectly, the typist inserts a fresh piece of paper in the machine, pushes a button, and the recorded text types out error-free at a speed of 150 words per minute. When revisions are necessary, the typist keyboards only the changes or additions. Unchanged text, already recorded, types out automatically.

Word processing systems utilizing this kind of equipment have been directly responsible for impressive productivity increases in countless offices throughout the country.

Telephone Switchboard and Booths

True nerve center of any office is the telephone switchboard or telephone room. In a small company the switchboard is usually located next to the reception room, so that the operator may do double duty as a receptionist. In a larger concern, the switchboard, manned by several operators under a supervisor, is usually located, along with a wiring rack room, in the service area of the office space, since its responsibilities do not require that it be convenient to any given department. Floor-loading requirements of the telephone rack room often demand special design and floor reinforcement because of the concentrated weight of the telephone racks. This special reinforcement of the floors to satisfy the layout requirements of the telephone company must be worked out with telephone company engineers. The telephone company has special planning departments throughout the country, which can be reached through business-office representatives, to assist with layout planning for telephone-service areas, for over-all telephone system of the office, for special facilities and approval of underfloor-duct installations.

It is customary in offices which do not permit employees to use office phones for personal calls to locate telephone booths at convenient places around the office so that employees can make such calls without going too great a distance from their desks. These booths should, when possible, be placed adjacent to semipublic corridors so that they can serve visitors as well as office personnel.

Filing and Microfilm Departments

Filing departments for active files should usually be centrally located, or at least located as near as possible to the departments generating the greatest number of records or having the greatest need to refer to records. This is fairly simple to establish on the basis of the work-flow analysis carried out by the space administrator in the initial stages of planning new office space. But if a company goes in for extensive microfilming of records, either in its storage area or in its central file department, certain specific requirements imposed by law on the microfilming procedure must be borne in mind.

Microfilm is noninflammable, but the law in many areas specifies that if any type of film is being used, it must be stored in fire-resistant vaults. Therefore, local building department regulations must be investigated when one is planning a microfilm installation.

In locating a microfilming department, it is important to ensure that there are enough electric outlets to feed power to the equipment, that there is good ventilation through the area selected, and that the floor will carry the weight of the equipment. Reinforcement of the floor is sometimes necessary.

Medical Services

Medical services in the modern office vary from the simple lounge area with a first-aid kit and a cot or couch to accommodate the indisposed worker to a complete dispensary staffed by doctor, dentist, and nurses. Although the medical facilities provided are, to a degree, a reflection of the corporation's attitude toward its employees, they are generally dictated far more by the size of the company and its location in urban or suburban areas. Some large offices in both city and suburban areas have medical departments as complete as small hospitals, with everything but operating tables.

Coat-room Facilities

Coat-room facilities vary from the extreme of a locker for each worker, through closets serving each department, all the way to open racks in exposed spaces for a number of general office workers. The most obvious, practical, flexible, and in terms of pilferage, safe arrangement is the standing coat rack, located where it can be seen by the group of workers whom it serves. Another arrangement similar to this, but presenting a neater appearance, is a wall wardrobe with sliding doors, located immediately adjacent to each departmental grouping.

The large coat room or locker room is not used so often today in city offices as these other two arrangements, since saving space is so important in terms of costs; either an open rack or a shallow wardrobe can be incorporated into relatively little space, while a fairly large area must be given over to a locker room or coat room. Moreover, theft is more prevalent in city offices, where there are a great number of visitors and open, unguarded stairwells, than it is in the country. For this reason, too, small wardrobes or racks within departmental areas may be preferable to large coat rooms.

In suburban areas, where there is comparatively little traffic from outside the organization and where employees enter the office directly from the outside, coat rooms right next to employee entrances may be desirable since they prevent mud and snow being tracked through the office areas.

Machine-tabulating Room or Electronic Data-processing Center

Machine-tabulating rooms or, in the case of very large companies, electronic data-processing centers, housing a computer and its associated equipment, pose special structural, mechanical, and physical problems in the office. With an electronic data processor, floor reinforcement is very often necessary and special electric power lines capable of carrying heavy loads are essential. The entire room must be soundproofed and isolated from the rest of the office and requires special air conditioning as well because of the heat generated by the equipment. Raised floors have been used for both air-flow and wiring. Very often there must be special treatment of the floor, beyond reinforcement, to reduce vibration caused by the machines. Machine-tabulating rooms require isolation from the rest of the office and special air-conditioning and soundproofing facilities but generally do not demand floor reinforcement.

Floor reinforcement, we feel, is most easily achieved through a "subway grating," a metal honeycomb framework set in a recess hollowed out in the floor slab and resting on the beams supporting the slab. This rigid grating furnishes a simple and perfectly effective method of floor reinforcement for most areas requiring it. Sometimes exceptionally heavy, concentrated loads, such as a giant computer, require direct reinforcement of steel beams and girders.

Recreational Areas

The larger the firm, the more consideration it will give to recreational facilities. For example, a firm of 1,000 to 2,000 or more employees might have its own cafeteria and lounge, library, game room, gymnasium, theater, and social hall. These would all be tied in with the personnel relations program and would be administered and directed by a full-time staff. The office staffed with 100 to 200 employees might provide a modest lunchroom or cafeteria next to a small lounge but normally would have no recreational services beyond this.

Cafeteria

Cafeteria, lunchroom, and snack-bar facilities again vary with the size of the office organization. If the corporation concerned has its plant adjacent to the office building, there are several different ways of handling the cafeteria program: (1) one large cafeteria serving both office and plant; (b) an office workers' cafeteria with a kitchen that supplies other food outlets for the factory workers throughout the plant; (c) in addition to, or as part of, the above schemes, a separate executive cafeteria or dining room where executives and department heads can eat privately with other executives or employees of the firm and with visitors.

Very often a lunchroom in either office or plant consists simply of a rack for a concessionaire to provide sandwiches, coffee, candy, and cigarettes. It should have table and seating capacity for employees who buy food and beverages, or bring their own lunch and buy a beverage from the concessionaire.

The snack bar consists of areas which might be located anywhere about the office, with attendants or simply with vending machines for beverages, sandwiches, sweets, cigarettes, and other products. Each of these areas, whether cafeteria, sandwich-and-beverage concession, or snack bar requires special planning on the part of the architect or space administrator. The advice of the food concessionaire or consultant would also be helpful in planning these areas.

Exhibit Room

Many office layouts include a company-product exhibit room. This is usually located near the reception area so that it is easily accessible to visitors. The exhibit room might be handled as part of a company office-service responsibility or be administered by the advertising or public relations department or by the sales department if it is in reality a show room or sample room.

Water Coolers

Water coolers are manufactured to serve groups of 25 or 50 people and are located within departments or in office corridors. The number and placement of coolers must be planned to satisfy the personnel groupings.

Recessed wall fountains serviced by a central water-cooling plant with unlimited capacity is an alternate method of providing drinking water. The location and number require detailed study in each case. Of late, the water coolers with both hot and cold water, which allow the office worker to prepare instant hot drinks, have become popular.

Clocks

Clocks are normally located in all departments. There should be one clock visible to each 25 to 50 office workers, depending on the office layout. Reception rooms, board rooms, and certain departments of the office have special requirements for clocks. Standard manufactured clocks may be separately connected to electric wall outlets, or all clocks may be centrally controlled and register the same time from a master clock.

Music

Many companies have loud-speakers throughout the office layout which are used as a call system or a speaker system for messages in addition to broadcasting music at planned intervals during the day. The music-control equipment is usually at a location convenient to a central communications center.

Machine-repair Shop

Depending on the size of the corporation office, various office machines and typewriters may be serviced by outsiders under contract or on call, or, alternatively, by employees. In the latter case a machine-repair shop is needed. This activity is usually part of the office stationery and office equipment and supplies department and requires special analysis for layout, equipment, construction, and storage facilities.

Library

The office library is centralized in the larger corporation, with all books under control of a company librarian. Special consideration is given to the secretary's and treasurer's department tax books, etc., as well as to the needs of the legal and engineering departments and others.

We must not confuse the office library with the employees' recreational lending library, which falls under the general heading of employee recreational facilities.

Here again special detailed planning is required in connection with library layouts for clerical control, tables and chairs for reading, book shelving, and filing.

Office Service Center

Often, many of the office services described above are combined at one central point for office service. An example of the arrangement of a typical corporate office's service center for each of several floors is shown in Illustration 8-7.

Service Departments

In addition to the above-mentioned facilities and services for the office, there are departments serving all other divisions of the company that must be planned in full, detailed office layouts. These are:

Personnel, for the recruitment, placement, training and morale activities of the office staff. Personnel often includes credit union activities.

Real estate, for the acquisition and management of real estate of the company.

Legal, to provide necessary counsel or act as liaison with the corporation's attorneys to satisfy all legal requirements of the company.

Accounting, to serve all departments in money matters and personnel payrolls.

Purchasing, to get bids, let contracts, and do all buying under specification and centralized control to satisfy company operations.

Advertising and public relations, to advertise and publicize the company's activities, both within the company and with the public, and to act as liaison with the company's advertising agency. The company's house organ would also be a responsibility of this department.

BUILDING SERVICES

Just as every office organization requires basic office services, so every office building incorporates service facilities. Some of these are musts—required by law; some are essential to the functions of the building; some are built in as conveniences, depending on the attitude of management and the size of the corporation.

These are structural facilities, built into the building as permanent features. Thus building services, in a tenant-owned building, must be integrated with the proposed layout plan for the ultimate efficiency of company and building. Building services consist of the following:

Building Stairs and Ramps

In a multistoried building, building stairs should be planned to carry much of the traffic load between any two adjoining floors. But to do this, stairs must be located in spots easily accessible to the personnel using them. Distances between building stairs should be about 100 to 150 feet to satisfy departmental traffic needs. Building codes set strict controls on the location of fire stairs, but these should not be confused with building stairs; the former are designed for safe emergency exit, the latter for convenient traffic patterns.

Ramps, which are excellent traffic arteries but which do require a lot of space, are found to be advantageous functionally and practical economically only when the corporation has an office staff of 1,500 or more and the building itself is not more than five or six stories high.

Fire Stairs

Proper design and placement of fire stairs and exits, including the provision of fire-retarding vestibules, shafts, and hallways, are a vital part of building and office layout planning. The pattern of egress should be approved by the local building inspector and fire department officials before any construction begins. All fire stairs should have an outer-air platform entry.

Toilets

Toilet areas, including powder rooms for women, necessary plumbing, and ventilation shafts, are considered part of the building-service area.

Elevators

In the two- or three-story office building, the conventional, individually controlled, self-service elevator is usually used to supplement stairways, ramps, and escalators. In the case of offices requiring multistoried buildings of five, ten, fifteen, or more floors, automatic self-service elevators are used. This self-service system puts all elevators under centralized control so that both peak loads and isolated calls receive prompt and efficient mechanical service.

Escalators

Escalators in the last few years have been used very successfully in offices in combination with elevators, stairways and ramps. The many combinations range from one escalator, serving two floors and reversible to meet peak loads, to two, three, or more escalators serving an entire building for vertical traffic at all times. These may all be switched to one direction during the morning, noon, and evening rush hours. Arrangements combining elevators, escalators, ramps, and stairs are now emptying buildings housing 5,000 to 10,000 people in five- to ten-minute periods.

Janitors' Closets

Janitors' closets to house porters' mops, pails, cleaning machinery, supplies, and porters' clothing should be located within the building-service area and as close as possible to general office space. Slop sinks are a necessity, and storage shelves to stock paper towels, toilet tissues, soaps, etc., should also be provided in these closets.

Freight Elevators

Within the building-service area freight elevators should be located either immediately adjacent to passenger elevators or near loading platforms and basement exits. They thus require special study and placement in the building-service core. In many smaller buildings, one or two elevators may serve a dual purpose, being used as passenger elevators during office hours and as freight elevators in early morning and evening hours.

Fire-protection Hoses

Fire hoses must be provided on each floor near fire stairways or building stairways, according to local fire department and building department regulations. They are sometimes supplemented by fire extinguishers. Fire alarm systems should be planned in conjunction with placement of fire hoses and extinguishers.

Pneumatic Tubes and Dumb-waiters

In many tenant-owned buildings, where all facilities are designed to meet the needs of the owner, pneumatic tubes and horizontal or vertical conveyor systems are planned to speed vertical or horizontal distribution of papers between departments and to aid mail distribution and collection. There are several manufacturers and types of equipment represented in each of these major physical-communications systems; when a particular system has been selected, the manufacturer can help plan an efficient layout of the mechanical-distribution pattern.

Watchmen's clocks

Watchmen's clocks are used as a check on the efficiency of the protection system against burglary and fire and also help to lower insurance costs for the building. Thus many office buildings today are equipped with the watchmen's clock system. As the watchman makes his inspection from floor to floor, and in given areas of each floor, he turns a key in each clock in sequence, which causes the clock to register the time of his check on his control or record card. This gives proof of maintenance of the guard service and the frequency of the checks for each area.

Such clocks or stations should be laid out in a pattern that will give management assurance that each building area is properly covered during the watchman's tour.

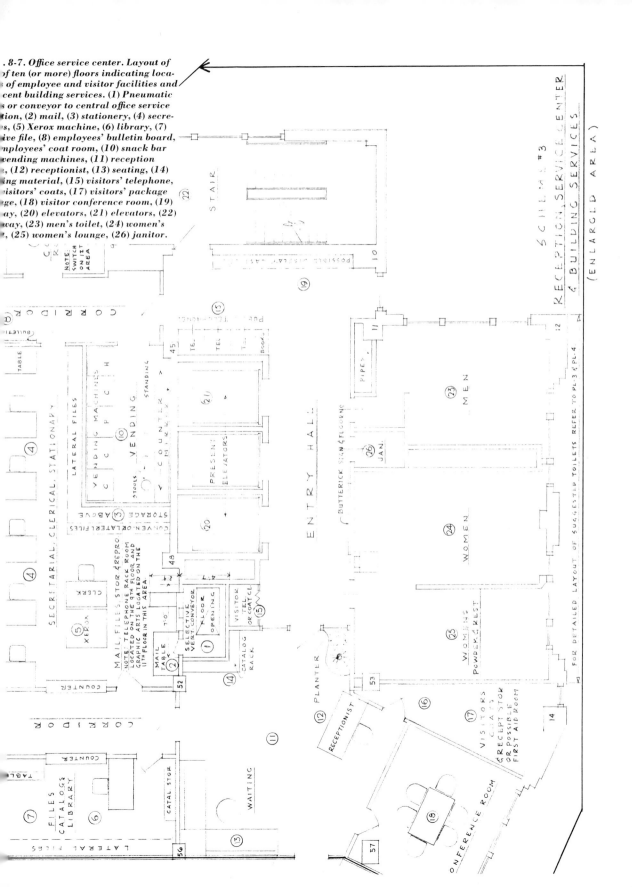

8-7. Office service center. Layout of ... of ten (or more) floors indicating loca- ... of employee and visitor facilities and ... cent building services. (1) Pneumatic ... or conveyor to central office service ...tion, (2) mail, (3) stationery, (4) secre- ..., (5) Xerox machine, (6) library, (7) ...ive file, (8) employees' bulletin board, ...mployees' coat room, (10) snack bar ...vending machines, (11) reception ..., (12) receptionist, (13) seating, (14) ...ing material, (15) visitors' telephone, ...visitors' coats, (17) visitors' package ...ge, (18) visitor conference room, (19) ...ay, (20) elevators, (21) elevators, (22) ...way, (23) men's toilet, (24) women's ..., (25) women's lounge, (26) janitor.

SECURITY (Watchman Services)

In the central security office of a large company there might be a closed circuit TV installation with cameras located at hallways, entrances, and exits. Most often there is a perimeter protection system for doors and windows, along with ultrasonic, photoelectric, or microwave motion-detecting devices that are connected to, and/or monitored by, outside protection agencies or local police.

Smoke detectors, activated by the presence of smoke, are recommended for computer rooms, refuse areas, and storerooms.

Perimeter protection and burglar alarms are often coordinated with card-key access. Every office should have its own specifically designed security system which is planned for by the office administrator and architect when designing the new office.

nine

SELECTING PARTITIONS AND OFFICE FURNITURE AND FACILITIES

It has been emphasized repeatedly throughout this book that the good office layout is the flexible layout in which departmental or personnel changes can be made with a minimum of inconvenience. But preplanned flexibility in the mechanical and physical elements of the office must be matched by equal flexibility in furniture and the nonstructural but relatively fixed elements of the office partitions. Recognizing this, manufacturers of the furniture and the partitions of the office have designed them in such a way that they contribute to the office's flexibility and lend themselves easily to any changes in the space plan. It rests with the office space administrator to recommend to management the furniture and facilities that best suit the company's office functions. It is in his interest to buy and have his architect include them in planning for the new offices.

Should it be to continue the conventional approach of Phase I, or to adopt screens as dividers as in Phase II, or to venture the new mechanics of wall-hung work surfaces and components of Phase III, or to go with Phase IV, the new proven method of architects, engineers, builders, and manufacturers of building material, furniture, and partitions featuring total modularity and open furniture and panelwalls.

Most important to the office space administrator is the continuous responsibility of daily satisfying space and furniture and office layout planning problems of his company, and this would suggest Phase IV with the new high-profile office furniture for open appearance in successful crowding and panelwall partitions for flexibility in layout. To achieve this, in-house custodial staff can be used.

Let us review the variety of choices of today in furniture and partitions by looking at examples of manufacturers' lines in each of the four phases described. Some manufacturers provide all four.

PHASE I. Illustrations 9-1, 9-2, and 9-3 show the latest conventional 60- by 30-inch double pedestal desks with complete flexibility of drawer sizes and types and with choice of overhanging desk tops for conference or added widths and matching accessory furniture. They are constructed of various woods or metal in various colors.

Illus. 9-1. Conventional desk.
(*Shaw Walker.*)

Illus. 9-2. Conventional desk.
(Right) front; (Below) rear. (*General Fireproofing Co.*)

Illus. 9-3. Conventional desks.
(Right) high profile; *(All Steel Equipment Inc.)* **(Below) double pedestal.** *(Steelcase Inc.)*

PHASE II.   Illustrations 9-4, 9-5, and 9-6 show divider screens, lateral files, and adjacent desks for use in open office layouts.

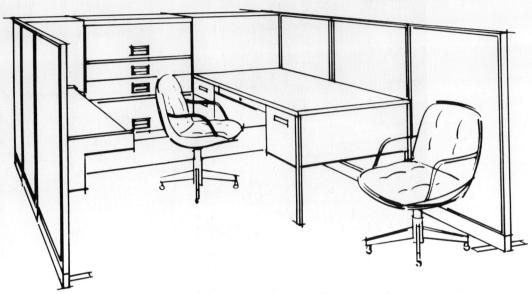

Illus. 9-4. Open office—screen and adjacent furniture. (*Steelcase Inc.*)

Illus. 9-5. Open office—screen and adjacent furniture. (*Steelcase Inc.*)

Illus. 9-6. Open office — screen and adjacent furniture.
(*Royal Metal.*)

PHASE III. Illustrations 9-7, 9-8, and 9-9 show divider screens with work surface desks and attached components for use in open office layouts.

Illus. 9-7. Open office—screen and attached components. (Westinghouse Electric Corp.)

Illus. 9-8. Open office—screen and attached components. (*Herman Miller, Inc.*)

Illus. 9-9 Open office—screen and attached components. (*Royal Metal.*)

PHASE IV. Illustrations 9-10 and 9-11 show today's open office panelwall partition and two-legged desk and related furniture.

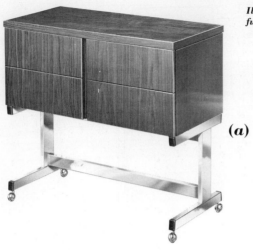

Illus. 9-10 (a)-(b). Open Office—open furniture. (*Cramer Industries.*)

(a)

(b)

Illus. 9-11. (a–c). Open office—
panelwall partitions.

(a)

(b)

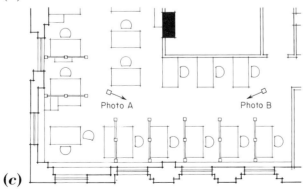

(c)

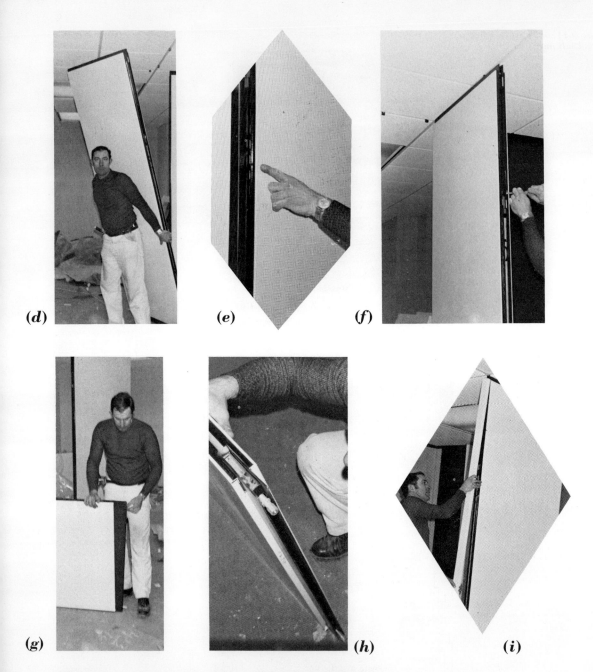

Illus. 9-11 (d–i). (d) Custodial staff relocating a lightweight section of panelwall after having attached ceiling module clips to the exposed T Bar of the ceiling suspension system. (e) and (f) Lifting lever for raising the ceiling channel over the ceiling module clips fastening the panelwall at the ceiling. (g) and (h) Movable telescoping base and floor leveling bolts for keeping panelwall in place (over the carpet or tile without fastenings). (i) Installing end cover plate for finished panelwall. (Courtesy E. F. Hauserman Company.)

The selection of a furniture and partition manufacturer's product today is more important than ever before because once installed and integrated with spatial conditioning, mechanics, and structure, they are maintained as the company standard for the life of the building or length of lease of the space.

Before 1960, departments in conventional compartmented offices were isolated by continuous floor-to-ceiling partitions, so that lack of standardization was not noticeable, and was an accepted fact. Purchases of furniture were often made as needed from the lowest bidder. This is not so anymore. Today with interlocking partitions and suspension of desk work surfaces, cupboard and file components and with partitions coordinated with ceiling modular design, a company must continue purchases from the company where the original furnishing order was placed.

This normally does not apply to executive suites and supervisory executive offices, but the continued expansion, contraction, and functional layout changes of the general office open areas require that panelwall partitions integrated with structure or divider screen partitions and their related component furniture be of the original furniture manufacturer's design if standardization is to be maintained.

PARTITIONS

The most important element in space flexibility, once space has been properly conditioned physically, mechanically, and structurally, is the non-load-bearing partition wall which can be moved easily. There is almost an infinite number of movable partitions on the market today, made of every type of material. There are partitions to separate clerical stations in the general office, and there are partitions perfectly suitable for the "walls" of the board room (see Illustration 9-12).

Most often, partitions employ steel, wood, or some composition for the main surface element. Modular panels which can be interlocked or secured by posts make it possible to construct a wall of any desired length of ceiling-height partitions. There are limits to the number of panels that can be linked together if less than ceiling-height partitions are used, since the wall formed by such panels cannot be secured at the top and so tends to become unstable if extended too far. This does not apply if very low parti-

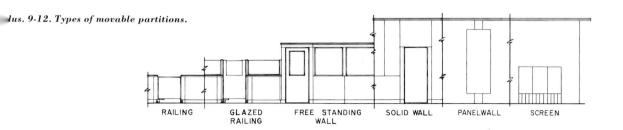

Ilus. 9-12. Types of movable partitions.

RAILING   GLAZED RAILING   FREE STANDING WALL   SOLID WALL   PANELWALL   SCREEN

tions—rail, dwarf, bank, or free-standing screens are used, since floor "shoes," "angles," or floor reinforcements can give such low units satisfactory rigidity.

Since movable partitions are available for every purpose and can be used to create handsome executive offices as well as every type of clerical and administrative office, they are fast replacing the fixed customary masonry walls of the past. Among the many advantages of panelwall partitions are:

1. Not only can they be moved easily, they can be taken down or put up quickly. Simple fastening devices make erecting a wall of any height a very easy matter that can be handled by regular office-maintenance personnel. (See Illustrations 11-d, e, f, g, h.)

2. Since the panels that form the partition wall have baked-on paint and other finished surfaces when they come from the factory, the long delay involved in waiting for a masonry wall to dry, painting it, and then waiting for the paint to dry is completely eliminated with prefabricated, factory-finished, movable partitions.

3. Partitions, since they are made of interchangeable modular panels, are completely salvageable. If a "wall" is taken down in one spot, the panels can be used to build a new "wall" somewhere else.

4. Most movable partitions made today are fire-resistant and soundproof.

5. A modular unit which combines a ceiling-high or low partition and a piece of furniture is also becoming very popular in the modern office. The integral desk-and-partition is in effect a miniature private office which can be moved bodily as a unit from one part of general office space to another.

The way partitions are used and the type of partition employed by any given office are closely linked to the interior design and atmosphere of the office itself. Every corporation has its own distinct personality, derived from its history, its traditions, its management, and the type of business it represents. We have said above that partitions are made today that are handsome enough for a board room; others are completely functional. The type chosen for a company's office standards program for various areas of the office will depend on the functional requirements of the office as well as on the particular limitations of the areas in which the partitions are used.

Illustrations 9-11a to i show the panelwall in use at a building's window wall where clear or opaque floor-to-ceiling glass might be used, and its moving by in-house staff.

Illustration A-7, in the Introduction, shows high-wall, low-screen, and wall components manufactured by the E. F. Hauserman Company.

FURNITURE

As we have noted, most companies today wisely insist on standardization of furniture, as far as sizes, designs, components, finishes, and accessories are concerned, at least through all ranks of the company up to the top officials. This not only gives the office a neater, more efficient look, it also aids planning, since the space administrator is working with known standard sizes of desks, tables, chairs, files, and other accessory furniture in his office layouts. In space rearrangements, he does not have to check to ensure that a given department's furniture and equipment will really match up or fit in the space assigned.

Basic desk size for most office workers is 60 by 30 inches, although individual companies may specify larger or smaller units according to their general inclination toward liberal or economical space standards. Economical standards could suggest desk sizes of 58 by 28 or 56 by 26 inches. With a 5-foot module allowing for a 10- by 15-foot office, 60- by 30-inch desks are compatible, whereas with 4-foot module, 58-by 28- and 56- by 26-inch desks are more in harmony (or scale) and keeping with the economical office space objective, here the 2-legged, high-profile desk can create an illusion of spaciousness.

It is common for offices to establish three different furniture levels for general clerical workers, middle-management executives, and senior executives, although company officers may be permitted some freedom in furnishing their own private offices.

Offices of the president of the company and other top executives, such as division heads, should provide the relief from basic standardization. Special furniture is often designed for these areas. Special-design furniture provided in more spacious and comfortable sizes might last the executive his company employment period, and many companies permit executives to retain their suites in retirement (see Illustration 9-13).

Illus. 9-13. (a–d) Office furniture of special design. (General Electric Company.)

(a)

(b)

(c)

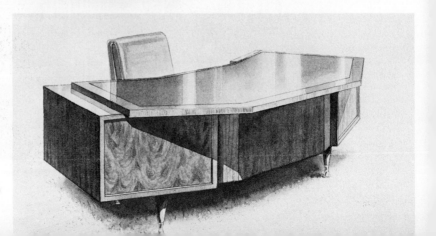

(d)

OFFICE DÉCOR
AND MAINTENANCE

DÉCOR

Most large corporations today stress the conservative approach in their design and décor. Smaller companies, or companies in which individuals *are* the business, are free to express a little more personality in design. Both groups are linking their product or products more and more with décor by displaying the product in board and reception rooms and by tying in company trademarks or the company's name with decorative treatment of public reception areas.

In decorative treatment of private offices, company policy varies widely. Some companies impose almost complete rigidity, giving every executive at any given level an office that is an exact duplicate of the office of each of his colleagues. Others give each man above a certain organization level almost complete carte blanche in furniture, color treatment, and wall and ceiling materials. The most common policy is a happy medium: top-level executives are given a choice of several different, harmonizing "office packages" so that they can express their own environmental wishes to a degree but cannot come up with an office completely different from that of every other person in the organization. Only in exceptional cases does a corporation give an executive a budget for free use in design and furnishings. At middle-management levels, almost all companies make an effort to have private offices as uniform as possible with varying furniture standards and colors.

Even in companies where the executives have a choice between several different office treatments, it is becoming more and more common to treat the president's and board chairman's offices in very much the same fashion as the quarters of other top company officials, except that the president and chairman may have larger offices for conference purposes and certain extra facilities.

The most radical changes occurring in office décor today are in the general office area. The drab, uninspired workshop of the past, jammed with every type of mismatched furniture, is becoming the exception among progressive companies. Today, the general office in a top company is brightly lighted, air-conditioned, and sound-controlled. Color is used freely, not only on walls and floors, but very often in furniture and equipment as well. Furniture, of course, is standardized and colors, where more than one is used, are harmonized. It is not at all unusual to find interior planting areas and good pictures on the walls.

The general office, in other words, is following the whole trend of American business for the past several years — to build more and more fringe benefits into the office job, to do everything possible to make that job pleasant and rewarding.

Color

The dull buff, once so drearily characteristic of clerical work areas, is passé in today's office. Pastel shades accented by occasional bright colors should be seriously considered by any concern planning the color pattern for a new office. Conservative organizations may feel that bright-color accents are a bit radical, but they will find that pastel shades make the general office a brighter and more pleasant place to work, without violating the character of the company. In private offices, bright colors can be used to great advantage and often offset the high costs of wood paneling and expensive decoration.

It should be remembered that in selecting colors for any office area, the amount of light at the source and its resultant brightness on the working area will be greatly affected by the colors used on the walls, ceilings, floors, and equipment. Thus lighting and color plans should be developed together. It is the pastel shades in any color that reflect light the best and can be used in unlimited combinations unobtrusively.

Two-tone color effects can be very pleasing, as the automobile manufacturers learned a few years ago, and today such color combinations are being carried over into the office. Light grey and green, or either shade with beige, make very effective color combinations for offices.

We quote from a talk by Mr. W. A. Fogel, a color specialist for the Pittsburgh Plate Glass Company, which has done a great deal to promote more imaginative use of color in the office.

> *Subconscious Effect of Color.* It is a scientifically established fact that every color in the rainbow has its primary associations. For every color there is some

one thing that is most closely associated in the subconscious mind. Thus, various colors are given definite functions in the field of color dynamics. Yellow suggests sunlight and warmth. Blue is a color calming and spacious in its effect. If incorrectly used, however, it can be depressing. Red is generally associated with danger, fire, excitement. Used with discrimination, its effect can be energizing. Too great a use of it, on the other hand, can cause irritation. Green can be characteristic of both its components—blue and yellow. Because of its association with nature and its eye-resting qualities, it has an almost universal appeal. Violet has the formality and richness of both red and blue from which it is derived. It has always been associated with royalty and luxury. Its practical uses are limited. Orange, being made from red and yellow, possesses attributes of both. It is the brightest and most cheerful of all colors. Except for tints and shades, it should be used sparingly.

Since color energy is a source of power, can either be a stimulant or a depressant, can help people relax or make them feel cheerful, the importance of choosing the right color not only with the eye but also with the head, becomes obvious. When you select colors which seem merely attractive, you may be forcing people to work in a room that is psychologically unsuited to them. Such surroundings may gradually get on their nerves, may affect their work or cause them to go elsewhere.

To quote further, this time from the Du Pont Company:

> In offices there are sound technical reasons for using different colors under different conditions. Room exposure should be a first consideration. Interiors facing east or north tend to be cool. To compensate, they can be "warmed up" emotionally through the use of such colors as ivory, buff, peach, or beige. When the exposure is south or west, cooler colors are desirable. These might be soft greens, greys, blues and blue-greens.

In large general office areas, business machine rooms, and drafting rooms, where most employees face in one direction, contrasting color treatment of an end wall can be highly beneficial. In this case, the wall which the majority of the workers face is painted in a color complementing that of the other three walls. This techique has been highly successful in areas where the work performed requires close attention to figures or details and so taxes the eyes.

It also gives a number of other practical and beneficial results. In the first place, it relieves glare and visual shock when employees look up. It provides a pleasing area to relax the eyes. And it breaks up the monotony of the entire room, since the area has a different appearance when viewed from different directions.

In private offices, color conditioning can accomplish a number of very specific and useful purposes. For example, the eye-taxing brilliance of excessive daylight can easily be reduced by choosing dark, cool colors for walls and ceilings. On the other hand, an office that does not have enough natural light can be brightened with color, even to the extent of giving it an effect of strong daylight. Again, through the proper understanding and application of color, a small office can be made to look larger, a narrow one wider, or a long one shorter. Even ceiling heights can be made to appear lower or higher at will.

Choice of materials for walls and floors is directly related to the choice of color. Heavy-duty areas need "heavy-duty" colors and construction. An office layout always has a semipublic corridor serving both passenger and freight elevators, halls, stairs, telephone and electric closets, and rest rooms. A serviceable color and material must be used for floors and walls subjected to busy corridor traffic. In most cases, we find terrazzo floors, in some color that does not show soil easily, and marble walls most practical; in spite of the wide variety of new materials for floor and wall coverings that have recently been introduced, nothing is more reliable than this time-tested combination, which competes with ceramics, quarry tile, and slate.

Flooring

There are four major factors to be considered in choosing the flooring for office areas. The first is the color and reflective value of the material being considered. The second is its resilience, third, acoustics, and fourth, cost.

We have found that linoleum, rubber, asphalt tile, vinyls, and cork are quite satisfactory for general office use. These materials are available in a wide range of colors and designs suitable for offices and are generally resilient.

Today, carpets are coming into more and more favor in many companies for general office use as well as for private offices. They offer distinct advantages: they have good resilience, excellent sound-absorbing qualities, and, most important advantage of all, are far easier to clean than the more conventional hard-surface office-flooring materials. Although they will not wear as well as linoleum and tile surfaces, the savings achieved in cleaning and maintenance will tend to offset the fact that carpeting must be replaced more often than the other materials.

Maintenance costs being an important factor in decoration, we see ceramic tiles on walls and floors of business offices, lobbies, corridors, and reception areas with and without the use of rugs (see Illustration 10-1).

Illus. 10-1. Ceramic tile floor and wall surfaces. (*American Olean Tile Company.*)

MAINTENANCE

One of the important benefits of flexibility in office planning, over and above its primary purpose of improving employee and corporate efficiency, is the fact that it eases the maintenance problem and cuts maintenance costs.

The benefit of good layout in simplifying maintenance becomes obvious through one example: adequate straight aisle space and a sufficient number of aisles and corridors simplify maintenance just as they smooth the traffic pattern in the office during normal working hours. If aisles are straight and long, with wastebaskets easily accessible, this one phase of the nightly cleaning procedure can run on the same efficient flow pattern that is ideal for any work process. If aisles through the office are wide enough to allow cleaning equipment to be moved easily, that, too, speeds the maintenance process.

But as in any other work procedure, the most important factor in the maintenance job is the personnel charged with the work. Careful selection of cleaning personnel may seem a trivial concern, but a moment's thought will show why some thorough screening should be done. First and most obvious, cleaning personnel have access to the office at a time when no other employees are present; it is essential that they be of good character. They should certainly be able to read and write, and it is an advantage if they are adaptable and capable of adjusting to new situations rapidly. Because of the nature of their work, it is important that they be healthy.

Cleaning may be carried out by building personnel, by employees hired directly by a tenant in a rental building, or by a contractor who takes over all cleaning services on a regular basis, either for individual tenants in a building or for a building as a whole. But, of course, cleaning is only one phase of the over-all maintenance problem, which also embraces various trades to ensure that building, mechanical, and electric equipment stays in good operating condition, that the building is adequately protected during the night hours, and that its appearance is fresh and attractive at all times.

In the case of a company which owns and occupies its own building, all these maintenance services are usually grouped in one department. Typical organization charts for such a maintenance organization for a small tenant-owned building and for a large tenant-owned building are shown in Illustration 10-2.

Maintenance procedures, like all other procedures in the office, should be spelled out in some detail for the personnei who are to handle them. All incoming personnel in any part of the maintenance department should receive the following initial training:

1. *Orientation.* They should be given a brief description of the work of the company, its basic purposes and products, and its general personnel and salary policies.

2. *Regulations.* They should, like any other employees, also be given

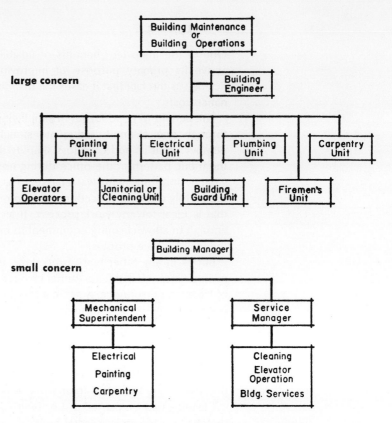

Illus. 10-2. Typical organization chart for building maintenance staff.

full and complete details on procedures for reporting to work, pay periods, and company regulations governing leaves and sickness.

3. *Detailed training.* Careful and explicit instructions should be given each worker on the assigned area in which he is to work, the exact methods by which he will do his work, and where he will keep his equipment and supplies. Such instructions, as far as cleaning personnel are concerned, will also cover the frequency with which different cleaning procedures are to be carried out.

Such a timetable for cleaning will vary with different organizations, but the schedule outlined below is fairly typical and may be helpful in arriving at your own program.

EVERY NIGHT

Empty wastebaskets
Dust ash trays
Dust desk tops
Dust table tops
Dust counter tops
Dust window sills
Clean mirrors (tenants')
Clean washbasins (tenants')
Clean coolers (tenants')

  Dust chairs
  Dust files
  Vacuum rugs
  Dust bookcases

ONCE A WEEK
  Dust desks, tables, and counters (except for tops)
  Dust lamps
  Dust pictures and accessories
  Empty pencil sharpeners
  Dust baseboards
  Dust doors
  Wet-mop tile floors—once over
  Wet-mop terrazzo floors—once over
  Dry-mop floors

Necessary supplies and equipment for all scheduled cleaning procedures should be stocked in supply closets at all times. A minimum supply list should include furniture polish, soap, drain flush, various types of waxes, and sweeping compounds. The equipment list should include a vacuum, polishing and scrubbing machines, wall-washing machines, mops, small trucks, sponges, floor brushes, dustpans, and an assortment of small brushes for radiators and venetian blinds.

Selection of the equipment can be based on a series of tests, but most organizations simply buy on a basis of known brand names. This procedure is as safe as any, providing the personnel follow instructions on proper use of the material or equipment.

Mechanical and Electric Equipment

Elevators and other mechanical and electric equipment must be checked regularly. This maintenance service is often handled by outside service organizations on a contract basis. If the work is to be done by the company's personnel, the men must be selected with great care. Valuable equipment can be ruined by unskilled or inadequately trained help.

When mechanical equipment is first installed, an instruction book is usually included that states the servicing instructions and periods when the work should be done. These instructions should be carefully followed.

Building Exterior and Landscaping

Maintenance problems as far as the exterior of any building is concerned depend largely on the materials used for the facing. If major problems arise, the architect should be called in to advise proper procedures for their solution. Minor painting and repairing can be handled by the company's personnel.

When a new building is built in a suburban area, it is fairly certain that a landscaping scheme has been designed for the structure. Any necessary changes in the design should not be left to the groundmen. Any revision needed—enlarging the parking area for instance—should be studied with the architect of the building or with a competent landscape architect, lest serious harm to lasting beauty happen.

Actual upkeep of the grounds, of course, is a responsibility of the company's personnel or of an outside service organization. In any case, there will have to be a regular schedule for mowing the grass, trimming hedges, cleaning sidewalks, and removing snow and leaves. Such a schedule, carefully worked out by the office manager in consultation with ground personnel, will pay big dividends in keeping the company's property looking its best.

Furniture-repair Space

Many large companies are finding it profitable to employ their own furniture-repair personnel. Generally, space for such repair facilities should be near a general furniture storeroom and should be equipped with the usual power tools and benches. It is usually unwise to attempt repair of large, especially complicated items; it's much better to send them to special shops.

A company that standardizes on wall-hung component pieces of office furniture will have to carry inventory for servicing repairs, rearrangements, and additions; also, if divider partitions or screens are used as a company standard, they will also have to be given storage space for servicing and office rearrangements.

eleven

SELECTING NEW OFFICE SPACE

The situation of the company that can construct its own office space to meet its own particular needs — both present and future — is ideal. But this ideal cannot be realized by every company. Many concerns must maintain their home offices in major cities, away from their manufacturing facilities, and most of these cannot even begin to think in terms of constructing a city office building or buying an existing building.

They must depend on rented space and must be prepared to make the various compromises that such space requires. But these compromises may be kept to a minimum if the company that is to occupy the space follows two simple principles — selecting the space that comes closest to approaching the ideal location and functional layout for its offices and then conditioning that space to tailor it to the company's specific needs.

These are the principles. How are they applied?

They can be applied by a series of simple, logical steps, even though too many companies have ignored the obvious pattern of selecting the best space and then conditioning that space to meet individual needs. Let's see what the suggested sequence of steps is.

First of all, obviously, the new premises must be large enough to meet the space needs of the corporation. We have outlined in the early chapters of this book how space needs both for the present and for a definite period in the future can be estimated by the company. The total area needed by the company to house its office functions and the optimum floor size for functional grouping of departments can be determined as outlined.

These are the basic factors. Now company management can decide in what general area it wishes to establish its new offices. If it is setting up its offices in a new city, it would call on the city planning commission, urban renewal groups, other firms in the city, and the chamber of commerce to determine the neighborhoods in the city that might be most appropriate for its operations, which areas are being developed, and which areas, if any, are most closely associated with its type of business.

If the new office is to be established in a city where the company has had long experience, the company still must decide whether it is to look for new space in the area where it has its present offices or whether it should move to an entirely different neighborhood. Is it important that it find a location in a "prestige" neighborhood? Should it seek space in a particular type of business district or trade center because of the nature of its work, near a post office, bank, shopping center, airport, golf course, or executive residential area?

These are all management decisions that must be made before the actual work of selecting a building to house the new office can begin. Once management has decided which area or areas would be acceptable, the company can list requirements both as to space and as to neighborhood with one or more real estate brokers. As their recommended proposals come in, each building offered is investigated.

This is the crux of the whole matter. For in investigating the type of space offered, the space administrator must bring his whole range of abilities into play. He must check the proposed space and building from the viewpoint of its adaptability to modernization or alteration, of the services offered by the building, of construction features which will aid him in making the most efficient office layout.

Let's see how it would work out in actual practice. Let's assume the XYZ company finds it is cramped in its present space and is housed in four different office locations and feels that for business purposes it wishes to move to a newly developed business area and consolidate its offices.

It follows through on the survey of present space and projected space needs as outlined in Chapter Three. It has its space administrator make rough layouts of the proposed new space arrangements. It finds its exact square-foot requirements for both present needs and expansion needs. And its management determines the general area or neighborhood in which it wants the new offices to be located.

The company's requirements are listed with leading real estate brokers, or, alternatively, an exclusive agent is appointed by management. Let's say the XYZ company has determined that its present and short-term expansion needs call for 100,000 square feet and that its long-term expansion needs amount to an additional 30,000 square feet. It wishes to locate in the financial district of its home city. So it has determined its total space needs and the general city area it desires. Its best layout plan indicates that certain functional groupings require a total of 40,000 square feet of space. Therefore, the building selected should have floor areas with at least 40,000 net usable square feet.

Given these requirements, the brokers or the agent will submit possible building locations for the new offices. These will then be visited by the space administrator and members of the space committee who will check on the general conditions of the buildings and the space offered.

They will check the space first of all for its adaptability—the ease with which it can be altered to meet the particular needs of their offices. They should investigate carefully the height of ceilings if an older building is being considered. Are the ceilings high enough to permit hung ceilings to be placed beneath them to conceal air-conditioning and lighting facilities and still leave $9\frac{1}{2}$ to 10 feet of ceiling height?

They should check the modular construction of the building. What is the column span of the building? Will it permit logical interior groupings or clusters of desks and work stations? Does it permit the desired space standards for private offices, or will it force changes and compromises in the standards? For instance, if a standard of 200 square feet has been selected for administrative private offices, a column span of 20 feet would be ideal, but 25 feet would create difficulties in layout and perhaps require more space.

In terms of the desired space standards, is the window arrangement suitable for perimeter private offices? If the column span is 20 feet, but there are five windows on 4-foot centers in each bay, division of each bay into two 200-square-foot offices will be difficult.

Is the floor construction cinder fill over a concrete slab, so that underfloor ducts may be laid easily?

Is the building on direct or alternating current? Are its main power feed lines adequate for the electric equipment the company has?

Are its service facilities grouped in such a way that a logical traffic pattern can be laid out for each floor? What is its window and inner space ratio?

Let's assume further that after such an investigation three different proposed sites seem to be satisfactory, as far as mechanical and structural features are concerned. The next step taken by the space administrator and office space architect is to make actual schematic layouts for the office organization for each of the three different locations and see which one comes closest to the ideal pattern in terms of exact departmental space needs and work flow. The one that comes closest to the ideal layout will be, all other factors being equal, the best site for the new office space.

This is, to a degree, of course, an oversimplification. Obviously, different rental costs, different building services, different locations even in the same neighborhood will all play their part in the final decisions made. But, in any event, no company should rent any space until it has followed through the steps outlined and made a working office layout for each of the sites that is being seriously considered.

Aside from the desirability of the space in terms of the exact needs of its office, the company should check a great many other things about each of the buildings which it is considering. What services does the building offer? Are elevator service and heat and air conditioning available on weekends and during evening hours, as well as during normal working hours? If not, what will these services cost? Does the landlord furnish cleaning services or is that the responsibility of the tenant? What proportion of the cost of necessary alterations for the office's needs will the landlord assume?

The importance of all these factors cannot be overestimated, and they should all be checked thoroughly. In the field of building services alone, conditions can vary so sharply between one building and another of the same general age that each elevator in the first is required to serve 50,000 square feet; each elevator in the second, only 30,000 square feet.

The degree of the landlord's financial responsibility in making necessary alterations is one of the most important factors to be considered in making leasing arrangements. In all negotiations with the landlord concerning alterations, it is wise for the company to employ its architect's services; he can be of invaluable assistance to the company attorney in drawing the particular clauses of the lease outlining the tenant's and the landlord's responsibility for necessary alteration costs and specifications.

Most landlords will condition space to a tenant's precise requirements if a long-term lease is involved. But, of course, if the landlord is to pay for alteration costs, the rent figure he quotes must be substantially higher than the rent he would ask if he were not required to condition the space for the tenant's requirements.

Thus it is important for the company preparing to lease space to figure its alteration costs carefully and balance them against the different rent figures it can obtain, to gain the greatest financial advantage.

Generally speaking, it costs approximately $15 to $25 a square foot to condition office space for occupancy. This includes installing all major conditioning features—air-conditioning, distribution ducts, lighting fixtures, hung ceilings, and underfloor ducts—partitioning, venetian blinds, floor covering, painting, executive washrooms, occasional lavatories, and water coolers.

With this average figure in mind, the company can work out its own formula to determine whether it is best to pay a higher rent and let the landlord assume all alteration and conditioning costs or do its own work and gain the lower long-term rent figure.

The company's financial stature, tax situation, cash position, and long-term economic plans will all affect its decision. For example, if a company rents 100,000 square feet of space in an older building, and can get a rent figure of $5 a square foot if it assumes its own alteration costs, $7 a square foot if the landlord pays for the work, it can very easily work out what is the most advantageous arrangement from its viewpoint. Total costs, assuming a conditioning cost of $20 a square foot, will be the same for the tenant over a ten-year period. If the tenant pays for the alterations, immediate outlay will be $2 million and rent over the ten-year period would be $5 million, making a total cost of $7 million. Alternatively, if the landlord pays for the alterations, and the company pays $7 a square foot, total rental costs over the same period will amount to $7 million (naturally these figures are given simply as an example). Interest on invested money would affect these figures.

Now if the tenant company has large cash reserves at the time of a new lease or move but is in a highly cyclical business, it would probably be best-advised to pay its own alteration costs and ensure a low-rent figure for the future. On the other hand, a company which does not wish to tie up a large capital sum but is fairly certain of a steady financial future would probably choose the higher rent and let the landlord pay for conditioning the space.

It is essential, whatever arrangement is finally decided on, that management use its own architect to help the company with its cost figures. The architect can give the most accurate estimate of what total costs will be if the company does its own work; he can protect management interests if it is decided to let the landlord do the work.

If the landlord is to be responsible for conditioning the space, it is vital that all commitments be spelled out precisely in the lease. Here again the architect should be called on by management to advise it as to what is customary as well as to help with the exact wording of the particular phrases of the lease that cover the landlord's alteration obligations.

In other words, the architect should function as management's technical adviser on all negotiations concerning alterations, just as he will ultimately act as management's agent in checking quantity and quality of actual alteration work as it progresses.

If the company decides to let the landlord make all required alterations to meet its needs, it should still use its own architect to make the working drawings and specifications, even if the landlord offers the services of his architect. The reason is obvious: the tenant's interests are best protected by a professional whose obligation is to the tenant rather than to the landlord.

Detailed working drawings and exact specifications are needed in conditioning existing space, just as they are in constructing a new building, although, of course, extensive building design and structural drawings are not necessary. Specifications, particularly if the landlord is responsible for alterations, should be precise; when the landlord agrees to alter space to meet the needs of a tenant taking a long-term lease, he agrees to use the materials and install them in the manner specified in the lease.

Thus management, to protect its own interests and ensure a satisfactory office project without controversy, must see to it that specifications are just as precise as they would be if it were constructing its own building.

twelve

MODERNIZATION IN THE OLDER BUILDING

Comparatively few companies today either need or can afford a new city office building. The skyscraper is an economic necessity in commercial city building, but few companies require as much space as it provides to house their office operations.

Thus the average company, when it decides on a city office, will think in terms of renting quarters. There are many different factors to be considered in selecting the proper building for the new office, and one of the most important decisions to be made by the company is this: Should it choose a new building which will mean paying a high rent, or should it select an older building where rents are lower and then go through a building modernization program?

There are many arguments in favor of the latter course. The over-all cost will be lower than the cost of renting space in a new building, if a long-term lease is taken by the tenant. There need be no compromises with modernity in conditioning an old building. Moreover, since extensive alterations in the older building will have to be made anyway in order to modernize it, the building, as it is conditioned, can also be made ideal from a layout viewpoint. In other words, an old building, or a given number of floors in an old building, may be altered so extensively that the tenant gains what is in effect a custom-made office, at less over-all cost than would be involved in moving into a new building. It may even prove practical for the company large enough to justify its own city office building to buy an existing building and modernize it rather than construct a new building. Even if the company is not large enough to require all the space in an existing structure, it could—and often does—buy and condition an old building for investment purposes and as a guarantee that its own expansion needs can be met in the future.

If a company buys an existing building and modernizes it for its own occupancy, and for some rental income as well, obviously initial costs will tie up a substantial amount of capital. The company, however, will have acquired and improved an income-producing property and will have custom-tailored offices with provision for expansion for itself at comparatively low costs once alteration costs have been amortized. And, in the long run, it always costs less to own space than to rent it.

Basically, a building consists of exterior walls, floors, columns to support the floors, and shafts housing essential building services. The new building and the old both have these main elements; everything else within either can be altered. Thus the major true difference between the new building and the old lies in floor shapes, location, and outward façade. And, although basic building design cannot be altered, the façade can. (See Illustration 12-1.)

Illus. 12-1. Modernization of older building. (a) Before; (b) proposed metal cladding; (c) proposed interior.(Atlantic City Electric Co.)

(a)

(b)

(c)

Moreover, the office buildings built twenty-five to fifty years ago had high ceilings to permit the greatest penetration of daylight and the freest circulation of air. Therefore, they are easily adaptable to installation of hung ceilings to conceal overhead lighting fixtures and air-conditioning ducts. Floors in such buildings are generally constructed with a cinder fill over the concrete slab—and thus offer no more problems in laying electric and telephone underfloor ducts than do the floors of the new building.

Older buildings are usually built around a central service core, or have service facilities on the periphery, it is true. But the fact is that most new buildings are also being constructed that way, in spite of the many arguments against such design in modern structures. So, even in terms of basic circulation patterns, the older building does not differ too much from the new structure. And, aside from the inconvenience of a central service core, the older building can even offer some advantages as far as good circulation patterns are concerned. Building regulations have become more rigid with the years; the new building must have setbacks at prescribed floor levels, so that floor area in the upper stories is considerably smaller than it is at the base. The older buildings suffer few of these disadvantages; if they have setbacks, they are not so frequent, and thus their upper floors offer almost as much space as the lower ones.

Let's see just what the difference is then between a new building and an old one that is to be conditioned. We can place high-speed elevators in the old building; we can air-condition it and sound-condition it. We can install any type of modern lighting and underfloor ducts that we wish. We can modernize the facade. We can reduce each floor to open space, tearing out all standing walls and partitions, and then build anew to achieve the best possible building floor plan and spatial conditioning.

The older building offers exactly what the new building does in terms of the fundamental factors, for office occupancy: in other words, enclosed and protected working space. We can adapt that space to needs just as easily in the old building as we can in the new, except that we will normally have to add such features as an air-conditioning plant and new electric service lines.

Moreover, older buildings offer one additional advantage that is becoming increasingly important in this age of automation. The steel structural frame in the older building was usually designed for a floor load of 100 pounds or more per square foot. Building code changes have reduced this requirement, so that many newer buildings have floors designed to carry 50 to 75 pounds per square foot. But now when so many companies are investing in electronic units that are extremely heavy, the greater floor strength that was mandatory in older buildings gives them another advantage over more recent structures. The office buildings being put up now are again installing floors with a heavier load capacity, just to accommodate the new electronic units, but buildings finished in the last few years do not have floors with the capacity of the structures built thirty-five to forty years ago.

All these factors make it important for any company planning to take new office space to consider well-designed, well-constructed, and well-maintained older buildings very carefully. Some of the particular things that should be checked in any investigation of an older building are:

1. Floor plan. Normally, the average older building with floors of 10,000 to 20,000 or 30,000 square feet has a good space-disposition plan, but it should always be checked. A central service core or a periphery service plan is to be expected. There may also be a court that can be filled in for additional space. But one should make sure that all net usable space is unbroken by badly planned service facilities and that a good basic circulation pattern can be planned for proper functional use of each floor. A good space-disposition plan is essential if extensive modernization is planned.

2. Ceiling heights should always be checked to ensure that there is sufficient room to install air-conditioning ducts over a hung ceiling while still maintaining a comfortable ceiling height. This would generally call for a distance of 11 or 12 feet between the floor and the underside of the lowest projecting girders on the ceiling as a minimum dimension.

3. Floor construction should be checked to ensure that conventional cinder fill is there so that underfloor ducts can be installed easily.

4. Columns and window modules must be checked. The structural framing of the buildings put up forty to fifty years ago was generally very similar to the column spacing in modern buildings, and the window modules generally allow the typical bay to be divided into two private offices, but these spacings should be checked before any final commitments are made. Generally, a column span of 20 feet at the perimeter is ideal, although interior column spans of 30 feet lend themselves to good general office layout.

5. Mechanical facilities. Check to ensure that shaft space is adequate to house any new elevators that may be needed, and check plumbing, wiring, vertical air ducts and chilled-water risers for air conditioning.

If the building under consideration has the basic features specified above, then it is worthwhile to modernize it. If the company taking space requires only a floor or two, generally it would not be practicable to consider modernizing the entrance and lobby of the building, but if the prospective tenant is a major corporation requiring several floors, it may be possible to induce the landlord, as a condition of the lease, to redesign the lobby and building façade so that the total impression of the new offices will be a good one.

Obviously, if the corporation buys an older building, the lobby—possibly even the façade—would be included in the building modernization program.

The public relations aspects of a new office are important, and this may be considered an argument against a company's renting quarters in an older building. Here again, however, there are many really sound reasons for choosing the older building. As we have pointed out, the building owner, if a major tenant is considering renting space, will very often redesign a building's entrance and lobby to improve the building's appearance. The tenant can achieve exactly the same type of office on the floors he rents as he would have in the newest building in the city. And, very often, if enough space is taken, on a long enough lease, he can make an arrangement with the landlord through which the building is renamed for his company.

thirteen

THE OFFICE MOVE

Moving an office from one building to another, or moving departments within a building, can be an orderly and successful project which needn't hamper the company's work in any way, or it can be a confusing and frustrating experience which puts the company days behind on its work schedule.

The difference between the successful move and the poor one lies in the way the preliminary planning and scheduling of the move are carried out. If a move is properly planned and organized, it is perfectly possible to move an office of 500 or more people, with all its machines and furniture, between the close of business on Friday and the beginning of the working day on Monday. Moreover, it can be done comfortably. Employees, briefed in advance on the location of their desk or work station in the new quarters, can go directly to work on Monday morning at the new location. The company will have lost no working time at all.

If a company with more than 500 office employees is moving from one building to another, it can schedule its move over several weekends. Thus, a given number of departments would be moved on one weekend and start work at the new location on Monday; another group, the following weekend, and so on.

Obviously, however, there are a number of problems involved in moving the furniture and working equipment of a large office and ensuring that every piece of equipment, every desk and chair, is put in the right place and ready for use first thing Monday. Moreover, the larger the company, the greater the problems. Each piece of equipment or furniture moved must be identified, located in the old quarters, and put in exactly the right place in the new. Electric and phone connections must be made.

So the greater the number of pieces that must be moved, the more detailed the moving timetable and the office layout must be.

TOTAL ORGANIZATION MOVE

There are two basic types of office move. The "total" move involves an entire company's moving from one location to another. The other type involves the movement of one department in a company to a location previously held by another working group in the company, a move completed within one building.

Of the two, the total move, strangely, is much simpler to plan and carry out than the interdepartmental move. When an entire organization is moved from one building to another, it is moving into space that has either been built or conditioned for immediate use. But when a department moves to a location formerly held by another department, very often it is necessary for the former department to occupy its space right up to the time the move is made. Thus the incoming group very often must begin work while alterations are still going on. This complicating factor, of course, is one of the major reasons for the built-in flexibility through physical, mechanical, and structural conditioning of space that has been stressed throughout this book; such flexibility makes it possible to rearrange departments with a minimum of upheaval.

Still, with all the flexibility possible through intelligent space planning, moving part of an organization will often entail more planning and time than a total organization move, unless it is possible to remove all personnel from the space that is to be reoccupied by another group in time to make all necessary changes before the new group moves in. If it is not possible to move present personnel out, usually construction work must begin while they still occupy the area. Even though such work can be scheduled for evening hours, there will be considerable inconvenience to personnel who must continue working in the space being reconditioned.

Obviously, in a move to either new space or reconditioned space, there must be physical coordination of electric outlets, telephone outlets, and all other mechanical and electric elements with the layout plan for desks, machines, and accessory equipment. This is achieved through previous coordination of the layout plans and the working drawings that have been prepared by the architect, all of which are needed by the moving contractor, telephone company, and electrician during a major office move.

Let's review the sequence of layout plans and working drawings during construction of new space or conditioning of old space to see how these plans and drawings play a role in the eventual move.

One of the first sets of drawings that management receives from its architect is an office layout plan of all existing furniture and equipment and its location in the quarters to be vacated. On this drawing will be noted where everyone sits at present, which desks have telephones, and the location of special equipment. These layout drawings will be used in identifying all pieces to be moved and serve as the tagging plan.

The second set of drawings that management sees shows the first proposed layout of the new space. After a number of conferences, these drawings will become reasonably fixed and indicate the exact location of desks, telephones, machines requiring electricity, and other equipment in the new quarters.

The third set of drawings shows the underfloor ducts as well as the office layout plan. The places where electric and mechanical outlets are needed are indicated so that when the move is scheduled, all necessary outlets for telephone and electricity will be in the right places for the placement of furniture and machines according to the layout.

The initial step in planning the actual move of the organization is to prepare a memo of *moving procedures* for department heads. This memo is developed by the person or group in charge of the moving project, and goes to the company officers for study, as well as to department heads. The memo outlines the important work, duties, and responsibilities which must be carried out by company personnel in preparing for the move, its date, location for departments, and time of arrival of movers.

Instructions must be complete, and requirements that are to be made of all employees must be spelled out in detail. In addition, specific personnel in each department will be given additional departmental responsibilities by their department head.

Preparation of these written instructions is usually the responsibility of the company space-planning committee, representing all departments of the company. This committee is charged with making all major decisions concerning the move, its scheduling, and which departments are to be moved first, if more than one weekend is involved. The committee also determines exactly what moving responsibilities are to be assigned to department heads and other personnel. The committee's decisions are all incorporated in written form in the "moving procedures."

After the moving procedures have been prepared and approved, department heads, operating as instructed in the moving procedures, assign the individual workers in their departments who are to be responsible for such departmental duties as tagging furniture and equipment before the move and who are to cooperate with the movers at the old quarters and at the new quarters by helping them place furniture and equipment in the correct location in the new departmental area.

Instructions in the moving procedures also cover such details as the proper tagging and marking of equipment and furniture and the correct handling of desks, chairs, boxes and bins, typewriters, trays, files, books, and all other items from inkwells to pictures and potted plants.

Here is a memo covering a move from several different buildings to one new location:

1. *In General.* The purpose of this memo is to acquaint the company's

personnel who will assist in this removal with their duties in connection with the operation.

2. *Moving Plans.* Moving plans for all office space have been completed. Sample sets of these plans are available for your inspection. At the time the tagging operation commences, suitable numbers of these moving plans and tags will be distributed to each department.

It is possible that the tagging operation (see below) will develop the fact that some files and equipment are not shown on the moving plan. The architect's representative who will be on the tagging operation will make necessary alterations to the moving plans to provide locations for such equipment, and the moving plans will be corrected to their final form. It must be assumed that these plans in this final form are to be considered frozen.

3. *The Tagging Operation.* A tag will be applied to every piece of furniture and equipment. The tag will designate the floor, the section of the floor, the room number, and the piece number to direct the furniture or equipment to its exact location. Tags are colored to correspond to the colored zones on the plans (see Illustration 13-1).

This operation will be carried out by the moving company's personnel with the assistance of our company's personnel and the architect's personnel. A tagging group will comprise:

a. A representative of the department who must be familiar with all desks, files, and equipment of his department and who must be available on a continuing time basis from the time this operation for his department begins until it is completed

b. A representative of the company's purchasing department who is familiar with all new furniture purchases, all furniture being refinished, and all furniture interchanged among company employes

c. A representative of the architect who will be responsible for proper room and equipment numbering and who will make any necessary alterations to the moving plans that may develop

d. The moving company's representative who will do the major work of applying the moving tags and be responsible for his men

It is the architect's recommendation, confirmed by the moving company, that this tagging operation for the four floors of the first move should not commence until two weeks before the date of that move.

It is the architect's suggestion that we start this tagging operation with one tagging group, and we feel that this one group can complete the job in the working days that will be available before moving day. Should it develop that a second tagging group is necessary, this will be organized as required.

Tagging of the packing cartons for desk contents will be done by individual personnel of the company at the time the cartons are packed by them. The room and equipment number which will designate their location in the new layout will be given them by their departmental moving supervisor as indicated on the moving plan.

4. *Moving Schedule.* The removal operation is presently scheduled as follows:

a. First move: occupancy of the 5th, 6th, 7th, and 8th floors—Friday, August 31 through Monday, September 3 (Labor Day).

b. Second move: occupancy of the 4th, 9th, and possibly the 2nd floor lunch room—September 14 and 15

c. Third move: occupancy of the balance of the 2nd floor—September 21 and 22

d. Fourth move: occupancy of the 10th floor—Friday, October 15th

e. Fifth move: occupancy of the 1st floor—November 2 and 3

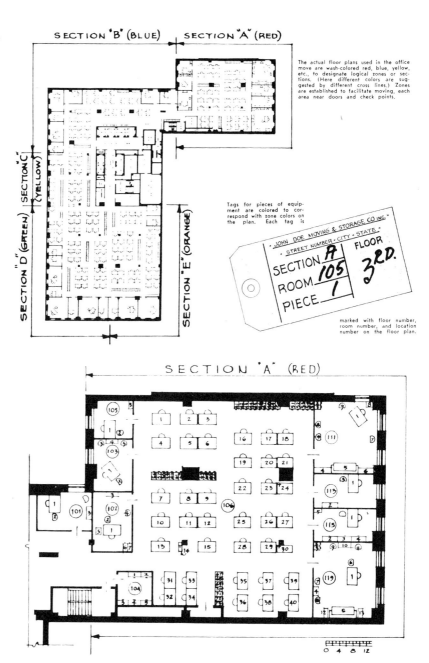

The actual floor plans used in the office move are wash-colored red, blue, yellow, etc., to designate logical zones or sections. (Here different colors are suggested by different cross lines.) Zones are established to facilitate moving, each area near doors and check points.

Tags for pieces of equipment are colored to correspond with zone colors on the plan. Each tag is

marked with floor number, room number, and location number on the floor plan.

The schedule of the first move for the Labor Day weekend is definite. The other four moves are tentative, and definite schedules for these will be confirmed seven days before fixed date.

The moving company has prepared a detailed departmental schedule of the Labor Day weekend move which is attached hereto.

5. *Company's Supervisory Personnel.* During the actual removal and oc-cupancy operation the following assistance will be required from departmental personnel:

a. One man who has been familiar with the tagging operation will assist movers in packing our furniture at the present quarters. If any tags have come off furniture it will be his responsibility to retag this furniture at the time of the move. It will also be his responsibility to inform movers as to disposition of any possible untagged material such as working papers, miscellaneous furniture items, machines, etc.

It would also be advisable to have a representative of the purchasing depart-ment at the present quarters at the time of the move. Knowing what purchases of furniture are contemplated and what furniture may be in the process of refinishing, he would be the person responsible for decisions as to what old furniture should be left behind, in the event that this question cannot be fully clarified at the time of the tagging, and what last minute substitutions are to be made. (Note: The tagging operation contemplates placing a different type of tag as a positive identification on all furniture to be left behind).

b. Two men who are familiar with the new office should be at the new quarters to assist movers and the architect's personnel in spotting the location of furniture.

Note: Alternates for the personnel having the above assignments should be provided in the event of illness. All personnel should be on hand an hour before their scheduled time in the event that the move gets ahead of schedule which often happens on a well-planned move.

6. *Liaison.* The company should designate personnel to act as liaison in making the following arrangements:

a. Necessary elevator services at all present locations—operators working overtime, protection of cars, and use of lobby

b. Use of elevators at the new quarters, as above

c. Disconnection of all telephones and other built-in or attached equip-ment like intercommunication and buzzer systems during the twenty-four hours preceding the move

d. Arrangements for moving any rented equipment to be made with the renting company

e. Telephone service between present and new quarters during the entire moving operation.

7. *General.* See moving company's *do's* and *dont's* and circulate same to all personnel concerned with the moving operation (see Illustration 13-2).

Any furniture or equipment from which the moving tags are lost in moving will be placed in a "Lost and Found" section to be established at the new quarters. Personnel whose equipment does not show up for the first working day should check this "Lost and Found" section for same.

Personal belongings will be moved by the individual, and the moving opera-tion will not be responsible for same.

It is tentatively planned that the company's personnel will be responsible for packing of desk contents only. Contents may be left in desks if they are packed solidly and drawers are secured. Other personal belongings will be packed in individual cartons provided by the moving company, which will be delivered to the employee's new work station at the time of the move.

All other packing of contents of steel shelving, stationery cabinets, and book-cases will be done by the moving company's personnel.

At the time the tagging operation begins, an office at the old quarters should be designated as "Moving Headquarters."

It's WRONG to do the following:

- ■ It's wrong to overload boxes to point of overflowing. Use extra box or container instead.

- ■ It's wrong to forget to tag every item. If an item comes apart, tag each part or section separately with the same number.

- ■ It's wrong to leave your personal belongings such as money, lighters, fountain pens, snap shots etc. in your desk. Take them with you to your new location.

- ■ It's wrong to place boxes or containers on the desks where they might scratch the surface. Leave them on the floor next to the desk where they can be conveniently moved by the mover.

Moving your office— Right and Wrong

It is imperative that movers have as much room to operate in as possible and it is our suggestion that only absolutely necessary personnel remain on the premises during the moving operation. Your moving cost can be materially reduced by efficient, split second timing and intelligent cooperation from each and every person. Moving day can be like any other business day, if you merely observe the following recommendations:

RIGHT

DESKS. Wherever possible desks will be moved with contents. Loose papers should be banded or placed in large clasp type envelopes. When moving, desks are turned on end to be taken out of rooms.

DESK ACCESSORIES. Desk lights, inter office communication systems or any other electrical equipment not requiring the services of an electrician should merely be disconnected from the electric socket and properly tagged using the number provided in the floor plan. Telephones attached to desks should be disconnected in advance.

LIQUIDS. Inks, mucilage, rubber cement and any other liquids should be removed from desks, cabinets and files. Be certain all tops, corks and stoppers are tight. Place in waste baskets or box.

FILES. Contents of file should remain intact with file guards drawn as tight as possible. Lock file if possible. Files will be moved upright whenever possible. Files fastened together will be separated by movers and replaced in new location according to plan.

CARDEX FILES. Rods and guards must be tightened as much as possible to hold contents securely. If there are loose cards, they should be banded together in packs of about 200.

TYPEWRITERS. Typewriters should be removed from desks and left on tops of desks. Tag typewriter with same number as desk. Typewriter will be placed in special typewriter box by the mover. Carriages should be securely tied.

STATIONERY CABINETS & STEEL SHELVING. Contents should be packed in boxes provided. Tag boxes with same number as stationery cabinet or steel shelving unit.

GLASS TOPS. Leave glass top on desk but tag with same number as desk. Remove paper or loose felt from under glass and place in desk drawer.

PICTURES—MAPS. Large pictures and maps should be tagged with new location numbers as indicated on floor plan and left on walls; small pictures should be removed from walls and placed in boxes marked with room numbers. All flat glass objects should be placed in boxes on end and not laid flat.

LOOSE CASTERS. If there are desks or chairs with loose casters, please remove same and place in desk drawer.

Illus. 13-2. Do's and dont's from moving company.

To complete the move smoothly and on schedule, both present and new landlords, building managers or superintendents must be advised as to how many building mechanics—carpenters, plumbers, steamfitters, electricians, and others—will be needed. Arrangements should also be made for telephone and electrical installers to follow up the movers to reconnect equipment that is attached to the desks.

A suggested form of specification for securing a competitive bid from a moving company could take the form of the following:

1. *General Scope.* The removal shall be carried out in accordance with the plans and specifications provided by the architect.

2. *Insurance.* Prior to commencing work the moving contractor shall furnish insurance certificates for the following coverage in approved amounts:

    Workmen's compensation
    Public liability
    Property damage
    In-transit insurance

3. *Responsibility for Damage.*

3.1 Lost or Damaged Articles. The moving contractor shall assume full responsibility for damage and/or loss of property of the corporation. Damaged articles shall be repaired or replaced as directed. Lost articles shall be replaced as directed.

3.2 Damage to Premises. The moving contractor shall assume full responsibility for damage to the premises above noted and to the new premises. Any such damage shall be repaired as directed.

Damage to painted and otherwise finished surfaces and/or floor coverings will be repaired at the cost of the moving contractor. Note: practically the entire new premises will be provided with new floor coverings, and particular care must be exercised to avoid damage to rubber-tile floor covering and carpets.

4. *Plans.* Detailed moving plans for all floors in the new premises will be furnished by the architect. These plans indicate placement of all equipment which will be identified by floor number, area designation and color, room number, and piece number (see Illustration 13-1).

5. *Inspection of the Premises.* All moving contractors shall tour the existing premises and the new premises and acquaint themselves with the scope of the work and the building facilities that will be required in the moving operation, such as elevators, basement lifts, loading platforms, access to the building outside normal working hours. The contractor shall also determine what payment must be made building personnel for work outside normal office hours and shall include these out-of-pocket expenses in his bid.

6. *Scope of the Removal Operation.* The removal operation involves vacating the existing premises, including a portion of the 3rd floor, furniture but not equipment in the telephone room on the 4th floor, and the entire floors 5 through 11 inclusive.

The operation involves occupying the new premises in all or part of floors 1, 2, 4 through 10, comprising some 125,000 square feet.

The 2nd and 4th floors will involve a small volume of transfer.

7. *Schedule.* It is contemplated that there will be a preliminary move into the 5th floor on a weekend prior to September 1, 1970, on one week's notice.

The major moves will be scheduled beginning, possibly, the first weekend in September, when three (3) additional floors will be occupied. Thereafter, two floors will be scheduled for moving on each succeeding weekend until all floors are occupied, finishing with the 10th floor.

It is understood that should certain department moves be delayed, they will be taken care of whenever feasible and not in conformity with set schedule.

All moves must be coordinated with the building management at the old and new quarters to avoid conflict with moves of other tenants.

8. *Moving Contractors.* The moving contractor shall furnish adequate supervisory personnel, as directed by the architect.

9. *Equipment.* The moving contractor shall furnish all necessary equipment, including vans, dollies, boxes, crates, rolling bins, hoisting equipment, packing materials, barrels, and other necessary items.

The moving contractor shall furnish specially printed tags conforming to the plan colors and with spaces for entry of floor, area, room, and piece number. The moving contractor shall provide numbered cards of proper color for room and area designations, as well as proper-colored directional signs with room and area numbers. All dollies and other wheeled equipment shall be serviced and in first-class condition.

10. *Protection.* The moving contractor shall furnish and place temporary protective coverings for walls and floors wherever required by the architect.

Protection shall include padding of elevator cars, if required; protection of floors, including street-floor elevator lobby and floor coverings, at points of heavy traffic; protection of threshold saddles; protection of the jambs of doors and marble corners at points of heavy traffic. Protection shall be furnished for all building and other surfaces involved in any hoisting operation. The moving contractor is responsible for securing necessary permits for weekend work.

11. *Preparatory Work.* The moving contractor shall carry out all necessary preparatory work prior to the several moves, as directed.

Preparatory work will include:

Preparation of detailed moving schedules, under the general time schedule set by the company.

Tag or poster identification of rooms and areas.

In open areas, the contractor shall be responsible for chalking on the floor correct location of furniture and equipment as shown by the office layout.

The delivery of boxes and other necessary equipment.

The unloading and packing of the contents of shelving. In the case of libraries, and wherever else directed, such contents shall be packed in boxes stacked on sides so that contents are available.

The shelving will be dismantled by others and then tagged and moved by the moving contractor. The shelving will be reerected by others.

General packing shall be carried out by the moving contractor, and this shall include all items to be moved, except the contents of individual desks. Each individual will pack the contents of his or her desk in boxes provided by the moving contractor. The moving contractor shall furnish and deliver approved skids at the new building for all safes and other equipment, as directed.

The moving contractor's schedules shall be timed to include necessary service work by others, including:

a. Plumbers for disconnecting and connecting equipment to be moved from old premises to new, such as water coolers, duplicating-department drain tanks, etc.

b. Electricians for disconnecting and connecting special machines and equipment which must be attached to desks and furniture

c. Carpenters for dismantling large pieces of furniture

d. Elevator service at both buildings, including a mechanic when necessary

This work will be arranged for by the architect, and the corporation will pay the costs of same.

12. *The Move.* The removal shall be carried out as scheduled, using the general transit procedure to be agreed upon.

13. *Work at the New Premises.* All equipment shall be placed accurately in accordance with the moving plans furnished by the company. The moving contractor shall pack all specified material at the present premises and shall be responsible for unpacking the same material after delivery to the new premises.

All boxes and other equipment used in moving shall be removed as quickly as possible. After all equipment is in place, the contractor shall "go over" the job and line up and straighten up.

Note: The moving contractor shall place all safes and other heavy equipment on approved skids.

14. *Time Tickets.* All time tickets shall be signed by a representative of the architect or the corporation, and a duplicate ticket will be retained by the signer.

It may seem surprising, but it is a fact that an office of 150 people can be moved overnight and a staff of 500 over a weekend with less confusion, error, and nervous excitement than is involved in moving a six-room household.

After a family removal, it generally takes several days before everything is settled, whereas the new office must be in working order at nine the next working day.

It is sound economy to plan an office move generally as herein described. Careless planning can create so much employee confusion and so distort and aggravate business operations that much time and money will be wasted.

fourteen

TO BUILD OR RENT —
CITY OR SUBURB

In the previous chapters of this book we have discussed the planning of offices. But offices can house 10 workers or 10,000; they can exist in two rooms in a converted city house; they can fill a city skyscraper. They can function as an integral part of a manufacturing complex at a major plant site; they can exist as an isolated entity in a primarily residential suburb of a large city.

In all locations, the principles of space planning and layout remain the same. But for many companies—though not for all—there are two primary decisions that must be made. These decisions will determine the basic structure housing the office and thus will affect very directly the way principles of good space planning are applied.

The decisions: whether to build or to rent space; whether to establish offices in the city or the country.

For many companies these questions never arise. The very small office is going to be located in rented quarters, unless it is constructed as an adjunct to the company plant. Most companies, if they decide on a city location, select rented quarters for the very simple reason that new construction in the city is usually not economical unless a multistory building is put up, and few companies need that much office space.

On the other hand, the company that decides to establish its offices in a suburban area may build its own office structure, buy an existing building and convert it for office use, or rent in an executive park or suburban office complex of which we now see many in our suburban communities.

As a general rule, the average company establishing its offices in the suburbs may buy, rent, or build; the average company locating its offices in the city will usually rent space.

This would seem to give an immediate advantage to the suburban office, since, as has been pointed out repeatedly in this book, the ideal office is the one that is designed for the specfic functions of a given company. And, since suburban land costs are relatively low, even a company of moderate size can think in terms of constructing its own suburban office building, which it cannot ordinarily do in the city.

The city-suburban question, however, even though it is accepted that a tenant-owned suburban office is more desirable from a functional viewpoint than rented space in the city, is not settled so easily. There are a great many factors which have induced many companies to move their offices from city to suburbs; there are just as many factors which have influenced companies—companies that have seriously considered a suburban location—to decide finally on remaining in the city.

Some of these factors will be outlined in this chapter through policy statements of two major companies, one of which moved from a city to the suburbs and one of which elected, after considering a suburban location, to remain in the heart of a downtown business district. But before considering the merits of the city office versus the suburban office, let's investigate the pros and cons of renting or building office space.

Obviously, the best arrangement from the standpoint of the functional operation of the office is to create a building specifically to meet the company's functional needs, to lay out space for the best possible flow of work in the company, and then design the building that will most efficiently house the proposed space layout. It is equally obvious that this is an economical and physical impossibility for many companies that must keep their offices in the city.

But what of the company that is just large enough to justify its own office building but isn't quite large enough to make it absolutely essential that it have its own building? If a company is in this position, it may very well recognize that its own structure would be ideal in terms of efficiency and prestige; it may equally well be very reluctant to tie up a large sum of capital in real estate.

When this is the case, the company can resort to a practice which is becoming more and more common in construction of major buildings today, the "leaseback." Under this plan a company can have its own building designed by its own architect. It will construct the building with its own funds, or with borrowed capital, and will then sell the completed structure to some financial organization or institution interested in real estate investments. It will then rent the quarters it has constructed on a long-term lease. The tenant may arrange to have title pass into its control at the expiration of the lease by paying a relatively high rent throughout the period of the lease or, alternatively, make no provision for ever acquiring title and gain a much lower rent. Although the tenant's yearly expenses for rent under either arrangement are considerably higher than its annual operating and depreciation costs would be if it held title to the building from the beginning, its working capital is not tied up in real estate, and it still has all the advantages of a custom-designed office building.

Naturally, the leaseback arrangement is not restricted to companies which plan city office buildings. It is equally possible for a substantial company to arrange such a financing device for a suburban property. The leaseback operates, in other words, to make it much simpler for any company which can justify construction of its own office space at all to achieve the best possible office structure for its needs, whether that structure is in the center of the city or in some rural area.

Even relatively modest offices with staffs of 75 to 100 employees can, if a suburban location is chosen, economically justify construction and ownership of a building over a ten- or twenty-year period. While a company with an office of this size would seldom think of constructing a new building in a city location, it can very often—and very profitably—purchase a small existing building in the city and convert it to meets its needs.

Of course, many companies cannot afford to consider a suburban location because of the nature of their work. A major bank is going to remain in the heart of a city's financial district where the greatest number of its customers and essential business contacts are concentrated. A major metropolitan newspaper cannot very easily be edited and published in a suburban location, although magazines can be and often are. But an office which serves mainly as a processing center, a clearing point for a national organization's paper work, can choose a suburban location and establish a successful office there.

The factor that determines whether any given company can successfully maintain its offices in the suburbs could probably be defined as the degree of importance of its internal operations as against its external operations. If the nature of the work done in a given office demands constant contact with other concerns, or with people from outside the organization, then the best location for *that* office is the point where it is most accessible to those other concerns and people. If, on the other hand, an office is more or less of a self-contained unit, carrying out clerical operations on data which come to it through standard communications channels, then a suburban office is perfectly feasible from a functional veiwpoint.

Assuming we are dealing with corporations which could choose either a city or suburban location, which is ideal?

The major arguments for a suburban location, as advanced by the companies that have moved away from the city, are that it offers a more pleasant environment than a city office, that it permits a more efficient building and therefore a better space layout than it is possible to achieve in the city, and that, to the degree personnel are isolated from other companies, it tends to reduce turnover.

The major arguments against the suburban location, offered by the proponents of the city office, are that it causes many inconveniences in dealing with other concerns, which tend to cluster in the city, that it creates serious transportation problems for both workers and executives, and that it deprives the company of the advantages of the large labor market that exists in the city.

Another argument less tangible than any of these, but one that is nevertheless advanced by many business men, is that personnel in a suburban office, through its relative isolation, lose the stimulus of constant daily contact with executives of other companies and organizations, that the suburban office is too apt to develop into a small, closed, company world.

Perhaps the most complete statements of the two points of view have come from the General Foods Corporation, which moved from midtown New York to White Plains, twenty-five miles away, and from the Mutual Benefit Life Insurance Company, of Newark, N.J., which decided, after considering seriously a suburban location, to build its new home office building in downtown Newark. Some ten to fifteen years have passed since these statements were made, but the reasons given here are still valid.

Speaking before the Office Executives Association of New York, Bertram B. Warren, General Foods treasurer, outlined these reasons for his company's move to the suburbs:

> My assignment is to relate to you the reasons which led General Foods to make its decision. These reasons seemed strong to us in General Foods, but they may not seem at all strong to executives of other companies, and in fact they may not even apply to the affairs of other companies.
>
> In our case the decision was to leave the Grand Central area and to locate, not in open country, but in a center of population within commuting distance of Grand Central.
>
> Our business home is set in a plot of 46 acres—enough to give us the living room we need, but a far cry from the country estate of hundreds of acres. Main thoroughfares pass our door. An airport is 10 minutes away.
>
> Three of us, a treasurer, a controller, and a personnel director, constituted the task force which reviewed some ten years of thinking about office locations and then put in more than a year of intensive survey and investigation.
>
> There is one other thought I wish you would hold in your minds as I interpret our reasoning for you, because it had a strong bearing on the solution. This task force was not asked to make a recommendation for 5 years ahead, nor for a 15-year lease. It was asked to recommend a location suitable to our needs 25 or even 50 years ahead.
>
> The improvement in communication and transportation facilities, the universal use of the automobile make possible a freedom of choice of office locations not possible in New York's earlier history. From this point of view, it is just as logical for offices to be located throughout the Metropolitan area as it is for department stores to take the merchandise out into suburban areas rather than to force the customers to come into the center of the city.
>
> Now for some of the more concrete reasons why General Foods chose a perimeter location—and White Plains specifically—over the Grand Central area where we have made our home for several decades.

First we agreed that the Grand Central area is unsurpassed in many respects. But it has come to have one great and growing drawback—congestion and its by-products—delay, inconvenience, dirt and noise.

We were trying to look ahead 25 to 50 years and it seemed to us that the trends of the last few decades would probably continue. If so, more and more people would be struggling into this limited area every working day, and out every night, increasing the congestion, the crowding, and the confusion.

These then are some of the reasons why we decided to leave Manhattan. To me they are not sufficient, alone, to be compelling, but they are serious enough to start one wondering if there isn't a better way.

The reasons for establishing our general offices in the County and in White Plains are legion, but there are two chief reasons, one affecting the company and the other affecting both the company and employees.

On the company's side, it has a deep conviction that, on balance, it can administer the company's affairs most effectively and efficiently from a White Plains location.

The employees are given a wide variety of practicable living conditions in addition to a work environment which for our purpose we think is excellent.

Let's look first at the office itself. Some of its advantages, such as air conditioning and fluorescent lighting, could of course be obtained in a new building in Manhattan. Others, such as lecture hall and cafeteria, could also be had in New York City, but at a steep price. Still others simply are out of the question in Manhattan.

The features I am about to mention, then, are desirable features which are part of low, campus-type office buildings but are seldom if ever found in multi-story buildings.

One of these advantages is the relative tranquility of the 46-acre landscaped site. The fact that the property has a view of distant hills adds to its charm. We expect that the added work enjoyment and pride all of us will have in a modern workshop devoted to our own business will reflect itself in morale and accomplishment.

An important feature to both company and employee is the modular construction of our new building which permits great flexibility in its use. Modular construction means the creation of a unit of space including a unit of floor, of wall, of window, of heating, of air conditioning. A building, then, is a grouping of these space units.

Offices are grouped in a few standard sizes, and everything comes out even, so to speak, as the standard-sized offices are laid out, in the desired sequence, along the side of the building.

As you can see, since virtually all of our office space will be utilized in open work space and four or five standard-sized private offices, capable of being arranged in any desired sequence, departments can be interchanged with a minimum of rearrangement expense.

Skyscrapers are not built that way. Usually economics and the building code dictate the size and shape, and the layout people take over from there, making the best of what they have to work with.

Since we are building close to the ground with no set-back restrictions, the widths of buildings can be arranged to give exactly the right proportion of deep space for open work areas, and perimeter space for private offices. In our case, we found that most of the buildings should be approximately 75 feet wide to give the right balance.

You must understand, too, that our three buildings are arranged in the form of a spreading letter U. The so-called number one building at the base of the U is 370 feet long and the two wing buildings are each 325 feet long. The wing buildings are joined to the number one building at the first floor level by passageways about 70 feet long.

Because of these dimensions and measurements, there is no waste or undesirable space. Every square foot of it will work for us.

The building is only three stories high and escalators are provided for passenger traffic. Consequently, space on lower floors does not have to be sacrificed to elevators for servicing higher floors, as is the case in multi-storied buildings.

All of these features of the site and building are peculiar to the so-called campus-type or garden-type building. They would not be available to us in Manhattan even if we were to build our own building. As our president wrote employees last April, "We see in this move an opportunity for greater job satisfaction for people. Many of the facilities we can offer in White Plains would not be possible in the congested Manhattan area."

So much for the working conditions. Now let's look at the personal side—the living conditions. Here there are two areas of benefit.

First, there is the wide variety of living conditions made available. Our move to White Plains, we think, places our offices in the center of that variety, rather than at one end of it.

Those who prefer completely rural surroundings can live north or east of White Plains and reach the office in a reasonable time by train or automobile. When the new bridge is finished near Tarrytown and Nyack, Rockland County and parts of New Jersey may find favor with employees.

It will be possible for employees to live in nearby suburban surroundings and walk or ride to the office, thus adding an hour or two to their leisure. Indications are that many employees will choose to live within 10 or 15 minutes of the office.

And a final reason why we chose White Plains. As we began to be aware of some of its advantages, we asked ourselves if there was a suitable site available, and we looked, and there was.

The other side of the coin, the argument for maintaining the office in the city, was expressed by H. Bruce Palmer, Mutual Life president, before the National Association of Building Owners and Managers:

A community is a place where people live together solving the normal social and civic problems of human affairs through their joint efforts. Here in this community they exchange goods and services in their pursuit of providing a living. They regulate human behaviour through the means of government. It has been of importance to our forefathers and it should continue to be important to us that our communities be maintained as the citadel of strength of our country.

A little history of our Company is in order also if we are to understand the decision which we made. Ours is a great financial institution which has been in business for one hundred and thirteen years. Thirty years ago we departed from the central city and moved about one and a half miles to what was then a residential locality. There we built an ornate and spacious structure noted for its beautiful Gothic pillars. This monument became a credit to the greatness of an institution but not to the efficiency of its operation. Our progress in sales had its ups and downs during this thirty-year period. We never wavered from out fundamental responsibility of security and service to our policyholders but our progress, in terms of expanded insurance sales, did not keep up with the industry. For this period of time we have been too much cloistered in our own existence. The area never realized its potentials, values of property declined and today it is no longer a desirable location for our type of business.

So we made our decision for progress. That decision dictated a fifty-year look into the future. We were importuned by many communities, as far away as Florida, to accept the services which they offered for our Company. Two sites were selected. One of these was in a suburban locality on a hundred and fifty acre golf course which we optioned for purchase. Word of this became public knowledge. The other site required careful negotiation, for it involved four and a half acres in the heart of downtown Newark. When some thirty different parcels of land had finally been assembled, we made our announcement.

The reasons, which I will outline below for choosing the urban locality, are personal and may not entirely encompass the thinking of our other Company directors.

1. *Taxes.* While some might consider these taxes to be high, they at least were stabilized and could be projected into the future as a part of long-time planning. The opportunity seemed apparent that increased ratables could be brought to the city, presenting the opportunity for tax reduction. Our city had a fixed plant with all services purchased and paid for. We would not be confronted with the problems of helping to finance services, an increased school load, police protection, fire protection, streets and all of the other services of the modern community.

2. *Labor.* We felt a definite responsibility for the happiness of our employee group. A move to the suburbs would have been disruptive to the established pattern of living of many of our long-service employees. We did not feel that they wanted to be hidden away in a beautiful valley or atop a scenic hill. Transportation services were quite adequate to bring our employees to this new place of business without adding a time element to be accounted for in the full day's effort.

3. *Importance of constant day-by-day relationships with the business community.* We carefully evaluated the broadening influence brought about by the participation of our people in community affairs. During the past five years we have each month brought into our Company outside speakers in order that our official group might not live entirely unto themselves and to our business. Decisions ranging far into the future cannot be properly made unless all of these broadening influences are constantly at work on the minds of men. For service to our policyholder group, the dynamic and competitive character of business today dictates the full usage of all of the modern service facilities of an urban locality.

4. *A maximum challenge to the opportunities of "good corporate citizenship."* To me this seemed the most important. Good corporate citizenship involves those things that can be done by a business, in conjunction with the principal objective of providing a needed service or product, that will help strenghten or improve the social or economic climate in which the corporate entity and its people work and live. Corporate citizenship also dictates constant attention to the care and welfare of those who are a part of the corporate entity.

And so the announcement was made with the largest headlines ever used in our local newspaper. With it came the thrilling experience of kindling a spark that was to be the rebirth of a city. But a spark will go out if it is not fanned. A meeting of fourteen of our leading business and industrial executives was called to coincide with the newspaper announcement. This was the charge we gave to these men. Your community will be only as great as the citizens believe that greatness to be. This community can be just as great as our vision of it today. Business is not a separate entity unto itself; it cannot withdraw from the rest of the community, for a community or a society to be great, the businessman must think great.

And so a new attitude was born from which we see the renaissance of Newark. No longer is there negative talk—no longer negative thinking.

fifteen

TYPES OF
OFFICE BUILDINGS

In the rapidly changing skyline of America's cities and across the face of its increasingly industrialized countryside, each new office building going up has a different life expectancy. Some of these buildings will live hundreds of years, as have the great buildings of the past. Others will be torn down like the buildings of a fair, will become obsolete in twenty-five to fifty years. Still others, built with glass and metal panelwalls or skins, may change their outer garb periodically, may have new surface materials applied, and thus be literally rejuvenated. Actually this new skin treatment is taking hold today and many of our largest steel companies and their fabricators are producing "metal cladding" designs and products by the mile.

A life of a hundred years or more? The skeptic may think that a wild exaggeration, especially in view of the office buildings we have been used to, which often seem outdated after thirty to forty years. Yet some of the structures being built today will endure because they represent a new and lasting concept of the office building. They mark the beginning of a new period of architecture, a period that has cut itself loose from the influences of the past to embark on new experiments in design, in the use of building materials, and in engineering techniques. The walls of such buildings may be literal "curtains" of light materials, hung from the structure's supporting steel skeleton, rather than the massive masonry façades of the past. Such construction makes these buildings as permanent as their skeleton, for their façades can be replaced. If they are correctly designed functionally, if they have been planned well enough to ensure the building's adaptability to changing times and needs, there is no reason why such buildings should not survive for centuries.

With modern materials and construction methods, rapid obsolescence or permanent value then becomes primarily a question of original design. If the building is functionally designed to meet current needs and is still flexible enough to be adapted to other needs in the future, there is no reason it should not be almost as permanent as the Pyramids of Egypt.

Technological improvements in the future may make parts of the building obsolete; changes in the area in which it is located may affect its usefulness and economic value. But a well-designed building will be one in which modernization of facilities can be carried out easily—and commercial neighborhoods change character slowly.

So—let's build our office buildings to last.

Naturally, the purpose for which a particular building is to be used will affect its design. A building that is built as a commercial venture ca not be designed to meet the particular functions of any given company, since it must be able to house a number of different companies, each with different requirements. It can be functional in design as far as structure, traffic, and facilities are concerned, but it will never be as fully efficient for any one tenant as a building designed specifically for that tenant, unless extensive reconditioning is done or the structure lends itself to the company's requirements.

A building is basically designed to shelter and house workers and their equipment. That is its first function. But various facilities required in a building may interfere to some degree with the workers' movements, may impose conditions on workers which hamper them.

Thus a building must have elevators if it is more than a few stories in height. If these elevators are housed in a center core, there is an obstruction rising through the center of the entire building, an obstacle which blocks free movement from one side of the building floor to the other. A worker in moving from one part of the office to another cannot always follow a straight line. (See Illustration 15-1.)

The truly functional building is the building which reduces these conditions to the smallest possible point, which places its service facilities so that they offer as little interference with free movement as possible, which has elevators, escalators, and ramps that can empty the building as quickly as possible. In other words, the most functional building is the building which offers as much unhampered interior space, quickly available from the outside, as possible, while still providing a comfortable atmosphere and protection from the elements.

And today, because of technological improvements, it is possible to build buildings which meet these ideals. Before air conditioning and the great advances in artificial lighting, it was important to get as many

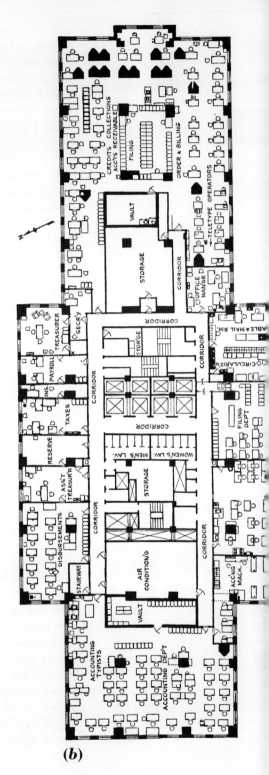

Illus. 15-1. Contemporary office building (core concept). (a) Building photo (Courtesy of Rockefeller Center); (b) floor plan (Courtesy of American Cyanamid Co.).

(a)

(b)

workers as close to natural light and air as possible. The dead center in a building designed under these conditions was the worst space in the building, the least habitable. It was natural and logical to house all the building's necessary service facilities in this center space, even though that imposed arbitrary and artificial circulation patterns on each floor of the building.

But with the development of air conditioning and artificial lighting that is in every way as good as natural light for office work, the distinction between interior floor space and space near the window walls vanishes. The entire office has the same temperature, the same humidity, the same lighting standards. Therefore, it becomes possible to design buildings free of the rigid conditions imposed on architects in the past by the necessity of providing natural light and air for tenants.

Under this new freedom, the truly functional building can be constructed—a building in which service facilities are housed in an area which is an appendage to the open floor space, rather than a block dead center in it. Such a building might very well take the form of the pictorial rendering shown in Illustration 15-2, where the center mass is all open floor

Illus. 15-2. Functionally planned and designed contemporary office building (service facilities appear as vertical elements). (Left) looking downtown; (Right) looking uptown. (Ripnen Architect, P.C.)

area, and toilets, stairways, elevators, shafts, and building machinery—all the service facilities of the strucutre—are housed in wings or appendages on each side of the center building.

This, to our mind, is the planning concept for the office building of today—the office building which can continue to function for generations since it has reached the ultimate purpose of such a building: the provision of absolutely free working space which is still protected from the elements. Even technological change will not make such a building obsolete, since all the technical and mechanical facilities of the building proper are housed in appendages servicing the center mass and so can be replaced or restored without destroying or altering the main structure which they serve.

Within this general context, however, the building designed to house a tenant's particular function has definite advantages over the building simply constructed as a shell or envelope into which many different companies, all doing different things, can be moved. The custom-designed building, which makes intelligent and imaginative use of the new freedom given the architect by the technological advances in air conditioning and lighting, is the real basis for truly contemporary architecture. Such a building imposes one additional demand on the architect, however. Since it is custom-designed to meet the particular needs of a particular company, it must be designed in such a way that it can continue to meet the needs of that company even if they should change. It must have built-in flexibility and adaptability, as well as a built-in preplanned expansion factor. The built-in flexibility is the total "interior environmental modularity" satisfying changes in functional office layout planning and its furniture and partitions without structural alterations.

TENANT-OWNED OFFICE BUILDING

The tenant-owned suburban office building usually represents the truest realization of ideal, functionally designed office space, because the architect has much greater freedom when designing a suburban structure than he does in the city. The tenant-owned city office building will almost always be a compromise structure because of the controls imposed on the architect by a minimum of land, site limitations, and city building codes.

By contrast, in suburban communities, sites are not arbitrarily bounded as they are in the city, nor do land costs make a tall building on a small site imperative. The open acreage permits the grouping of functionally planned buildings designed for the most efficient flow of paper-work operations. Moreover, suburban building codes are usually far less rigid as to building size and shape and general structural and mechanical designs than is the case in the city.

SPECULATIVE OFFICE BUILDING

The owner of a speculative office building must plan his structure for maximum income and minimum original investment costs. A variety of factors that do not handicap or control the architect of a tenant-owned rural building affect and, to a degree, control the final building design.

Often the building is constructed on an unusually shaped site which has been assembled through purchases of several small adjoining properties. This often results in an irregular shape. Of course, the speculative office building also must be planned for an ever-changing occupancy and thus can never be designed to meet individual needs as can a tenant-owned building.

The speculative office building, therefore, is never quite as efficient from the tenant's viewpoint as the tailor-made building, nor should anyone expect it to be. The true success of the speculative building is represented by the income it produces for the owner or sponsor of the building, not by how well the building works for the tenants. Naturally, there are qualifications here; if the building is highly inefficient, it won't have any tenants at all, or at least it won't have tenants prepared to pay premium rents. Thus, to be a success, the building must be as efficient as possible, within the limitations imposed by its being designed to meet the needs of different companies equally well. Experience shows that the acres of speculative office space being rented are those wherein the office space between the ceiling slab and cement floor is left to the tenant's architect to design spatial conditioning. In most cases the standards desired for the tenant are far above what the building owner has established as his building standard, and it is here that costly negotiations start in upgrading the specifications of the "work letter" of the office lease.

INVESTMENT TYPE OF OFFICE BUILDING

The investment type of office building is usually designed and constructed for a specific corporation's occupancy, or, on an unusually valuable site, for multiple-tenancy use, with one tenant occupying most of the building space. Many large institutions, such as banks, insurance companies, railroads, and large foundations, occupy such buildings, which are usually quality structures and may often incorporate special design features to meet the needs of the principal tenant. Here again, however, the limitations of the urban site and the extreme flexibility which must be built into the structure because of probable changes in tenancy result in a building only relatively efficient in terms of space use. The principal tenant is forced to compromise office layout planning and over-all architectural and engineering design to meet city conditions and to ensure the building's usefulness to other tenants.

Designing the building around the concepts realized in Illustration 15-2, the concepts which were described earlier in the book, will make such a city structure as efficient as possible. You will note that the floors in this design are open, free areas of good size and shape and that vertical transportation and building services are housed in appendages outside the main floor area. Such an arrangement gives the greatest possible degree of freedom for office layout planning on every floor, even though the needs of the company located on one floor may be totally different from those of its neighbors above and below.

CITY, STATE, AND FEDERAL GOVERNMENT OFFICE BUILDINGS

Government office buildings are almost invariably high-quality structures. In fact, they are so well constructed, even though sometimes poorly planned, that the building often outlives the original plan and design concepts of the year in which it was built. Like other urban office buildings, government buildings have to be planned for what is, in effect, an ever-changing tenancy. Organization structure is constantly changing in city, state, and federal government, and flexibility to accommodate such changes should be built into the structure.

Government buildings pose special problems to the space administrator, since they are not torn down as obsolete commercial buildings might be. Thus they must be modernized, which is often a major operation since so many of them were built before air conditioning or the development of modern lighting methods. Many government structures, for this reason, were built around large open courts which, with modern technological advances, are now unnecessary. The filling in of such open areas represents an obvious move for government to make and can expand tremendously the net usable space of present buildings. Industry has been doing this, and a good example is the Borden Building in New York City.

SUMMARY

When one is building an office building in the city, its plan and design are controlled by circumstances which force the architect to compromise his design. Physical limitations are placed on the building design, not only by the size and shape of the plot, but also by city zoning regulations. It is quite obvious that any preplanned office layout will be limited by these factors and that whatever layout is finally made will be controlled by them. In the suburban community, the architect will have ample acreage for his site and will have maximum freedom to create a building or complex of buildings that will permit the most efficient work flow. The limitations imposed by topography, orientation, and local building codes will be minor compared with those faced in a city location.

It is in the tenant-owned suburban office building that the concepts and principles described in this book may be most fully realized.

With harmonious grouping of the various functional elements of a structure, adequate service facilities, use of quality surface materials that will endure, and tasteful, ornamental embellishment, we have completed the ultimate office building.

This is the truest expression of contemporary office architecture, the building designed by, as well as for, the functions it houses. Such a building may take a variety of shapes, but its exterior form will be a faithful reflection of interior functions.

sixteen

BASIC OFFICE BUILDING SHAPES

Assuming that we plan to build our own building, how do we progress from the planning of interior space to the final design of the building?

In the design of new office buildings there are several basic shell arrangements which can be used to advantage. The most common are shown in Illustration 16-1. They are the simple rectangle, the L-, E-, I-, U-, and square O-shaped buildings, and finally the extremely functional design of a large, rectangular general office area with attached expandable wings for executive and special-service areas. Still another possibility is the pentagonal type.

Where the size of the site area does not limit the floor space of the building, which is generally the case in a suburban area, the horizontal height of the building should not exceed five floors in any of these basic building-plan types. In city locations on the other hand, where building density and land costs are both high, a rectangular or square shape with a number of floors will usually prove most economical and efficient.

The rectangular-shaped building is one of the most common units in architecture. Generally, a rectangular-shaped building is also one of the easiest to lay out and to build. If such a shape is adopted, it should be laid out so that there are at least two appendages for building services. Illustration 16-2 shows a typical arrangement for such a plan shape.

Another excellent building plan is the E-type shape. This arrangement

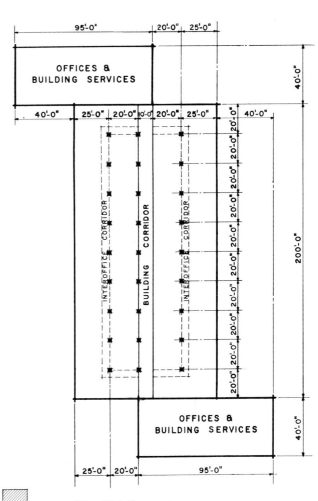

Illus. 16-2. *Two service areas as appendages to office building.*

Illus. 16-1. Basic building shapes.

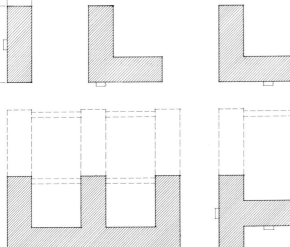

may start as an L-shaped building. As additional space is required, additional preplanned, symmetrical building units are added. By the same token, the L-shaped, by the addition of one unit, can become a basic U- or F-shaped building. A plan may start as an E-shape, with expansion needs being met as they arise by simply extending the wings of the building or by adding floors.

Among the many advantages offered by the E shape, particularly in a suburban setting, are that it offers maximum natural light and window space, departments may be expanded or contracted very easily, executive-office space can be segregated completely from general office space if that seems desirable and office space identification and office space administration are simplified.

The basic shapes discussed might be termed the conventional architectural plans for a suburban office building. But today there is a growing feeling that the plan shape must follow the interior functional requirements, must be, in effect, a package or shell enclosing the interior layout plan that is most efficient functionally for the company. A typical example of a building in which form is derived from interior function is shown in Illustration 16-3. A suburban building planned as an expansion of the above concepts for total functional flexibility is shown in Illustrations 16-4*a* and 16-4*b*.

Illus. 16-3. Functional office building showing preplanning for expansion.

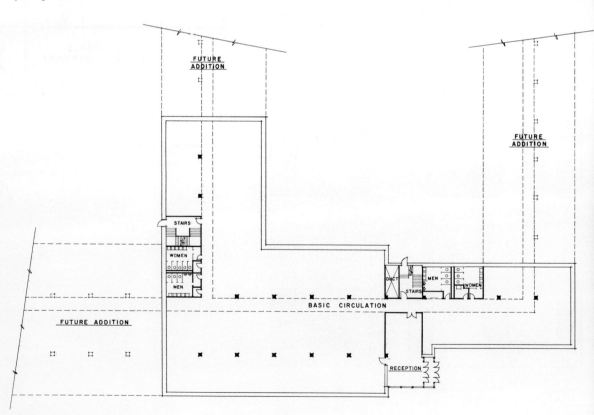

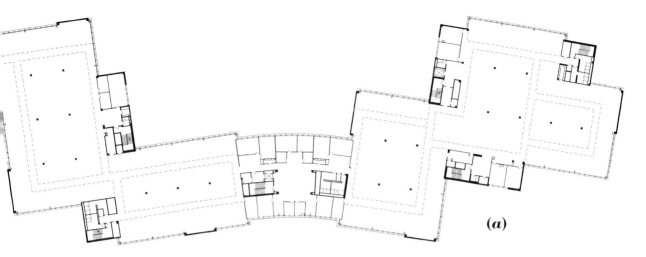

(a)

(b)

Illus. 16-4. A suburban building
planned for total functional flexibility.
(a) office layout plan; (b) exterior view.
(Courtesy Eggers Partnership.)

Multifloor skyscraper-type buildings, as mentioned earlier, will usually be based on some modification of the rectangular or square shape. Most such buildings are speculative, designed for maximum rental appeal, and therefore offer some drawbacks to any company as compared with a tailor-made design conceived to meet a given company's exact needs. But even with this characteristic of speculative buildings taken into consideration, most of them share one common mistake which is not necessary: They usually have only one utility core, placed, as its name implies, in the center of the building. This will always present departmental work relationship and circulation problems on each floor area, since the center of the floor is blocked out entirely by building-service facilities and the usable area is restricted to a wide perimeter around this core. To go from the southwest corner of such a building to the northeast corner it is necessary to go halfway around the entire building. Moreover, because of the break in open interior space created by the location of the building services, departmental expansion or contraction is made more difficult, as is the circulation pattern between departments. In short, the flexibility of office space for a tenant occupying one or more floors is compromised when a center-core building is used. Fortunately, we are beginning to see more buildings where a good functional space is left open and services such as elevators, stairs, corridors, and shafts are appendages to the building as shown in Illustration 16-2 and expanded in Illustrations 16-4a and 16-4b.

If a company constructs its own building, either in the city or the country, actual future physical expansion of total space must be planned for at the time of initial construction. In the city office building, the arrangement will usually be the same as in leased quarters; reserve space will be rented to other tenants on short-term leases. In a suburban area, the expansion will sometimes take the form of construction of floors or wings added to the basic building (see Illustration 16-3). Such additions should be planned for in the original architectural design of the building, and interior layout plans should be drawn showing how expanding departments will move into the new space as it is made available (see Illustrations 16-5 to 16-8). Suburban expansion space is sometimes built and sublet as in the case of rental of urban expansion space.

Illus. 16-5. Office building office layout plan before expansion.

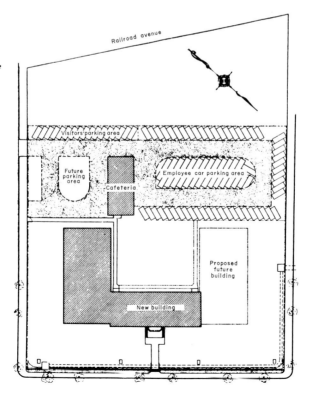

Illus. 16-6. Office building site plan before expansion.

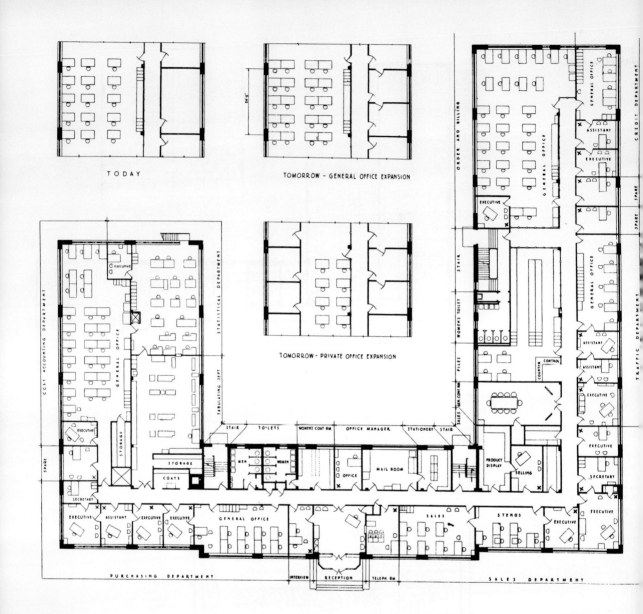

TODAY

TOMORROW - GENERAL OFFICE EXPANSION

TOMORROW - PRIVATE OFFICE EXPANSION

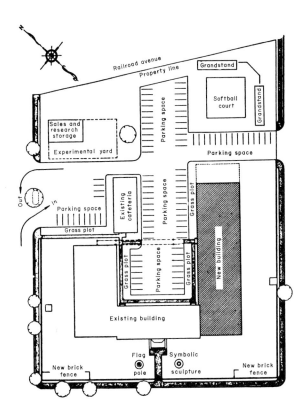

Illus. 16-7. (opposite) Office building office layout plan after expansion.

Illus. 16-8. (above) Office building site plan after expansion.

seventeen

CHECKING THE SITE

The ideal office building is a complex of many factors. But no matter how talented the architects, the planners, the engineers who create it, it will never be any better than its site. Therefore, the first step in creating a good building is to select a site of the right size, the right proportions, the right location.

Site selection requires intelligent study by qualified people of the requirements of the proposed building and of the people who are to work in it. These requirements are then used as criteria against which every potential site may be measured.

In effect, a checklist of requirements must be made. Then every site studied can be checked against each of the points on the list to see whether it satisfies the company's requirements. No matter how good a site may look at first glance, this procedure will ensure its being right for a particular company's needs.

Some of the questions which any company planning an office building should use as tests for a potential site are:

ACCESSIBILITY

How far must employees travel to get to work? The shorter the distance the better, of course. In a city with good public transportation, this is not so important a question as it can be in rural areas, but even in the city, the site selected should be as close as possible to major transportation lines.

If the office is to be located in a suburban area, the availability of public transportation becomes extremely important not only for employees but for visitors as well. If there is no public transportation nearby, the company may have to establish its own bus transportation to the nearest center. All these factors must be taken into account when estimating cost and desirability of a site and annual operating costs.

In the suburban office, too, relative accessibility or remoteness of public transportation will affect the size of the site that must be taken. If public transportation is inadequate, large areas will have to be devoted to parking space for employee cars.

Last of all, since employees must get to work and get out again at the end of the day, the site should be considered in relation to the main arteries nearby. Is it possible to design entrance and exit patterns from the site which will allow employees to drive between work and home with reasonable ease, or is the site jammed against a heavily traveled main road, so that several traffic bottlenecks are apt to develop in the morning and evening as employees try to feed their cars into a steady stream of traffic? Bumper-to-bumper car travel soon develops if poorly planned parking and inadequate egress roads hamper a site.

ENVIRONMENT

In either city or suburban setting, the surrounding neighborhood is a vital factor to consider in choosing a site. What kind of district is the proposed building site located in? Is it an area that is on the downgrade or one that shows every probability of becoming more desirable in the future? How are adjoining properties used?

Not only the quality of the area but also the actual physical conditions of the area should be appraised in judging any site. Are there industries nearby that create smoke, unusual amounts of dirt, unpleasant odors, and noises? Not only will such conditions make working at the site unpleasant—they can even constitute a health menace. Moreover, unusual amounts of smoke or dirt from adjoining areas will make maintenance bills for the office property skyrocket.

Even with the soundproofing qualities offered by modern acoustical treatment and by filtered air conditioning, which permits windows to be kept closed the year round, it is still important to locate an office building in an area that is relatively quiet—"quiet" here including normal traffic sounds, which are acceptable. Location near a fire station, where sirens or bells will distract personnel continually, or near railroad tracks is to be avoided where possible.

The site should be checked for unusual obstructions nearby which would reduce the amount of natural light available to the building. Even with all the advances in lighting techniques that have changed our architecture so radically, it is still advantageous to have as much natural light as possible for employees. By the same token, the site should be checked for unusual obstructions which would interfere with the view from perimeter offices. One of the factors that should always be considered in judging any site is the possibility of developing pleasant natural vistas for the people who are to work in the building. In suburban offices, too, the site should be judged from the viewpoint of landscaping possibilities—the higher the site the better the landscaping. And a high site solves drainage problems.

SIZE

One of the most obvious things to check in any potential site is its size. Naturally, no one is going to consider a site that is inadequate for the proposed building. But a site just large enough for the building is not adequate. The prospective owner must also ask if the site in a suburban area is large enough to allow sufficient parking space near the building and good approaches to the building; in the city, if there is some separation from adjoining buildings. In suburban areas the most important factor of all is allowance for expansion of facilities if that becomes necessary and for locating the building on the site remote from future disturbances.

ORIENTATION

Shape of the site in terms of the building plan is also an important factor. Is the site both large enough and of the proper dimensions to allow a building to be oriented to gain full advantage of the sunlight and the prevailing breezes of the area? Does it allow enough room, if it is a suburban building, for planting trees to give maximum shade during the summer? The orientation of the building is one of the most serious problems in locating any building on a site once it has been selected. Poor orientation in terms of sun and heat rays can mean unnecessary air-conditioning operating expenses throughout the life of the building; good orientation can keep such costs to a minimum.

TOPOGRAPHY AND SOIL

In considering various possible sites for a new office building, the wise buyer doesn't automatically eliminate the irregular, rolling piece of ground if it is offered. A good architect may actually be able to take advantage of such a site and give the client more space for less money. The lowest floor, built into the hillside, can often be an ideal location for housing mechanical and some service elements of the building and office departments, with less than the usual excavation problems.

If a rolling site is selected, the wise builder will bear in mind that it is better to cut away crests and build on firm soil than it is to backfill a stream, river, or valley and build on unstable ground.

Soil should always be checked on any potential site that is being seriously considered before any final commitments are made. Test borings will indicate whether the soil is sufficiently stable to hold up the proposed structure without unusually costly footings and foundations. Soil tests will also indicate whether or not landscaping will be successful, since trees and shrubs will not grow in poor soil.

Finally, the test borings will indicate how expensive a proposition it will be to build road approaches to the building and to ensure a proper drainage pattern for the entire property.

In the first stages of its search for appropriate sites for a new office, a company should get in touch with the local city or metropolitan planning and development commission. These commissions have as their function the creation and execution of a master plan for the continuing physical, economic, and social development of an entire metropolitan area. Thus they are able to provide information on future plans for any given neighborhood—streets to be cut through or widened, bridges to be built, creation of nearby water or air transportation terminals, and additional public transportation facilities to be provided.

Detailed information on public utilities, whether publicly or privately owned, is available from the planning commission, as well as data on site use, bulk and height of buildings, and trends in real estate values for any given area. The commission will also provide estimates on future population growth in various parts of the metropolitan area.

Thus proper use of the facilities of the planning commission can guide a company in determining the best city district or suburban region in which to carry on its intensive search for a building site.

When various potential sites within the desired area or areas are being measured, each of them should be checked for these factors:

1. *Size.* Is the site large enough to accommodate:
   a. The proposed building *and* any preplanned wings or additions to the building?
   b. Necessary automobile parking and recreation areas, if a suburban site is chosen?
   c. Roads and sidewalks, if the site is suburban?
   d. Necessary landscaping?
2. *Relation of site to services and labor market.* Does the proposed site offer:
   a. Nearby banking services for personnel?
   b. Nearby shopping areas for personnel?
   c. Convenient public transportation facilities?
   d. A fairly sizable labor market within reasonable distance?
   e. Good highway facilities if the office is to be located in the suburbs?
3. *Physical facilities of the site.* Will the proposed site offer:
   a. Easy access to power, steam, gas, plumbing and sewage, and telephone facilities?
   b. Freedom from any subsurface problems as indicated by test borings?
4. *Topography and soil.* Does the proposed site have:
   a. Firm soil which will support the building weight without unusual structural foundations?
   b. A plot outline which will allow the best possible orientation of the building?

These, then, are some of the major questions and considerations which must be kept in mind as alternative sites are evaluated. Most of the questions can be easily answered when the proposed building is to be constructed in the city; when a suburban office is planned, however, thorough investigation by experts may be necessary to check on many of the points outlined above. But in either case, the points mentioned should be used as a checklist against which every proposed site can be matched.

It is never wise to skimp on size in selecting a site. Size will, in the long run, probably mean more to the corporation than any of the other factors. Land is always the smallest part of a building construction budget in suburban areas, and the greater the amount of land surrounding the building, the more the building itself will be enhanced. Even in urban areas, where land costs are high, today's trend is to reserve some open space in the building plot, to enhance the building by giving it its own "breathing space" and improve the corporate image.

COMMUNITY IMPACT

What to seek in checking a site has been outlined, but there are items which any community planning commission would investigate when application is made for permit to build. Normally, before purchase of land an option to buy is negotiated. This is subject to approval and consideration of the following:

Physical — water supply, gas, electricity, sewerage, pedestrian and vehicular circulation systems, land-use, and city planning

Social — housing, schools, libraries, city hall, stores, shopping centers, religious buildings, and clubs

Economics — police, fire, garbage collection and disposal, community services, and tax base

Environmental — air, water and land pollution, e.g., potential traffic pollution of nearby residential areas may result in refusal of a perimt to build.

A suggested check list is as follows:

SITE EVALUATION CRITERIA

ACCESS
IMMEDIATE VICINITY
- Street width
- Traffic volumes and characteristics
- Turning movements and signalization
- Parking and other traffic controls
- Public transportation
- Possible access points to site
- Known plans for improvements
REGIONAL (EMPLOYEE AND CUSTOMER ORIENTED)
- Driving time to population centers
- Road capacity and future highway improvements
- Availability of public transportation
UTILITIES
AVAILABILITY AND CAPACITY TO SERVE THE SITE
- Water supply
- Storm sewers
- Electricity
- Communications
- Estimated cost and timing for providing same
- Sanitary sewers
- Gas
- Heating
SITE DEVELOPMENT FACTORS
- Size
- Topography
- Drainage
- Natural Features, Vegetation, Conservation Factors, Views, Appearance
- Zoning of site
- Condition, utilization of existing buildings
- Shape of property
- Soils
- Tree coverage
- Space for expansion
NEIGHBORHOOD DEVELOPMENT FACTORS
- Existing development pattern in the immediate area and district/trends
- Zoning of the surrounding area
- Relationship to community's master plan
- Community and neighborhood factors
- Availability of supporting commercial and industrial activities
- Availability of supporting educational, cultural, and recreational activities
- Housing
LEGAL AND OTHER IMPEDIMENTS
- Deed restrictions
- Easements
- Other government programs and restrictions affecting the site
- Need for zoning changes
LEGAL AND OTHER IMPEDIMENTS, ACQUISITION COSTS FOR ALTERNATIVE SITES, TIMING OF PROJECT DEVELOPMENT, OTHER CONSIDERATIONS

(*Courtesy Haines, Lundberg, & Waehler.*)

eighteen

SELECTING THE ARCHITECT

Simple logic shows that the organization planning a new office building on such extensive conditioning of space as we have outlined in the preceding chapters must have an architect to plan its layout, interior and exterior design and facilities, and supervise the work done by contractors.

Basically, space planning for the office organization in an existing building is a matter of deciding what can and what cannot be done within the existing structural frame and then working out the best possible layout in terms of the floor plan that is available. Basically, this is an architect's job rather than a decorator's or a contractor's. Only the architect, by training and experience, is able to think in terms of changing the interior building plan and spatial conditioning where possible to help achieve a better office layout, changing layout where essential to accord with the structure of the building, its stairways, elevators, toilets, and mechanical elements.

This is obvious enough when an entire building is being modernized. But, although not so obvious, it is just as true even when fairly extensive changes are being made on only one or two floors or in larger offices generally. Suppose it were possible to hire a contractor directly to install underfloor ducts, another contractor to put in air conditioning, and an office equipment firm to put up movable partitions. In that instance, unless the company has a comprehensive layout plan of its own, which takes into account all the various factors of new building or modernization and reconciles them all with the central plan, each of the contractors would be more or less working according to very rough and general directions from the company. The result would be exactly the type of broth that is always associated with too many cooks.

Even if the company did have a good layout plan, unless it had someone prepared to draw working plans, write specifications, and then supervise the entire conditioning job, each contractor would have to rely on his own judgment to a certain extent, and the result would be an office that might work but that would never be the smoothly functioning mechanism that can be designed by one architectural firm with the help and advice of the company space administrator.

The architect acts as the creator and director of the plan and its execution, the interpreter who translates the wishes and needs of the company into the technical language of the contractors who do the actual installation work. He also acts as the coordinator, the person responsible for seeing that all plans for each type of installation are in agreement with each other, that each contributes its part toward the whole and works together with the other facilities to give the best possible office.

There is another cogent reason for choosing an architect to act as the company's agent in all new building and reconditioning work. It is implied in the very term "agent." An architect has nothing to sell but his knowledge and his services; he is forbidden by every rule of his profession to have business relations with anyone other than his clients. When a company hires an architect, it can be sure that every piece of equipment he specifies, every installation he recommends, every new facility he advises is not only harmonious with the over-all plan but also the best equipment for the company's purposes, a necessary installation, or the best facility for the company's requirements, based upon the architect's training, knowledge, experience, research, and objectivity. Any design organization which solicits business by stating that it has an architect on its staff is breaking the law, since this constitutes the "sale" of professional services by a nonarchitectural organization. This is illegal for both the architect and the organization that employs him.

And, last of all, in addition to the obvious advantages of having one architect direct the over-all planning so that all elements of the office plan work together and are in harmony with each other, the fact that the architect is an artist as well as an engineer is reflected in the finished office. If the right architect has been chosen, the office will not only be functional, it will be attractive as well. Layout, partitioning, lighting, air-conditioning, and area masses will have been planned to make best use of the building structure and floor plan and to be, as well, harmonious in form and proportion with the building's interior structure. An architect's responsibility is not only the erection of a sound building with a pleasing façade and site but the interior functional layout of the building, the proportion of room and areas, and the "livability" and "workability" of the complete structure.

Where does the company go to find the right architect for its needs? How does it select the best-qualified architect among several being considered?

There are two generally accepted methods of choosing an architect: by direct selection and by competition.

The second method is seldom used except in the construction of public or special projects and offers some disadvantages for the average company since the choice of an architect through competition, according to the rules of the American Institute of Architects, must be made by a jury of judges who consider various designs submitted by architects and choose the one they believe best. The owner is then bound by the decision of the judges and must contract with the architect they have chosen.

The first method, direct selection, is the one almost universally used in private building. Although companies sometimes select an architect solely through knowledge of his reputation, it is generally safer to make inquires about the work done by several different architects and then select a group of those who seem most qualified to plan, design, and supervise construction of the type of building the company has in mind. These can then be invited to submit statements of their training and background, with descriptions and photographs of some of the work they have done, particularly work similar in nature to the project proposed.

The owner can then further investigate each architectural firm by direct contact with the companies for which it has done work and supplement this by personal interviews with the leading contenders. In these the owner can question them further and, just as important, determine what his personal feelings are toward the architect. For, after all, owner and architect are going to be linked together in a close working relationship over a long period of time, a period in which the architect will be the specialist and advisor and the owner will have to depend on his guidance through a whole sequence of technical details. It is essential that there be a feeling of mutual trust and respect between owner and architect.

In order to get a list of architects qualified to design a given type of building, a company may always request the suggestions of the local chapter of the American Institute of Architects, or write to the Institute's national headquarters in the Octagon Building, Washington, D.C.

In *The Handbook of Architectural Practice*, published by the AIA, the nature of the relationship between architect and owner and the safeguards the owner should take in choosing the architect for his project are spelled out in detail.

Free planning and designing in offering architectural services are barred under the mandatory rule of the AIA.

The *Handbook* goes on to say:

The Owner should give careful thought to the selection, since his interests depend so directly upon it. The Owner commits the expenditure of his money to the Architect, and though he may think he is in control of the situation, he is in a large measure helpless as to the way in which it is spent. In fact, he depends for a successful result almost as much on his Architect as does the patient on his surgeon. It is, therefore, of the utmost importance that, before reaching a decision, he should make careful inquiries along several lines, as for instance:

(a) Has the Architect under consideration the experience necessary for the work in hand?

(b) Has he the technical knowledge needed to control the design of the highly complex structure and equipment of a modern building, and to secure the best results without waste of space or money?

(c) Has he executive ability and the force to compel the proper preformance of contracts?

(d) Has he successfully done work of like character or work from which his ability properly to serve the Owner may be inferred?

(e) Has he such honesty and incorruptibility as are essential to the Owner's safety?

In brief, has the Architect established to the Owner's satisfaction his fitness, above others, to design the work and to control its execution?

As an aid to the direct selection of an Architect, the Owner sometimes invites several to submit statements of their training and qualifications, with a list and photographs of their more important works, as well as references to those for whom they have erected buildings. With these before him, the Owner, either alone or with professional advice, makes his selection; after all some projects require the relationship of Owner and Architect to extend over a period of three to five years and longer.

Last of all, after all these checks, if two or three architects remain, the company can ask itself one simple question about each man considered: If he were applying for a top echelon job within our organization, would we be eager to get him? If the answer is yes and the architect's other qualifications all meet the company's needs, if his previous clients endorse him and his previous work shows an understanding of similar companies' needs and requirements—then the right architect has been found.

The space administrator should not be asked to interview and invite architect's proposals if top management is going to select others than those interviewed. This often happens in the business world and leads to confusion and an unpleasant relationship.

The architect-owner agreements are described under the heading "Contract Documents" in Chapter Nineteen.

nineteen

WORKING DRAWINGS
AND SPECIFICATIONS

Whether one is modernizing an existing building or building a brand new structure, once the over-all plans and design have been created and approved, the process of preparing working drawings and specifications is much the same in the detail work: the careful preparation by the office space administrator and the architect of detailed working drawings and specifications are necessary to show the building contractor the extent of the work involved. The working drawings outline in graphic form the exact location and quantity of each of the various facilities that must be installed in the new building or the modernized space. The specifications spell out the precise method of installation to be used and the quality of the materials and equipment that must be used in each part of the new office.

Working drawings are usually prepared to a scale of 1/4 inch or 1/8 inch to the foot. They show locations and types of walls and partitions, structural frame and floor construction, electrical layout and controls, heating layouts, ventilating and air-conditioning layouts, telephone locations, water coolers, clock locations, plumbing facilities, etc.

Specifications for an office layout refer to and describe the way in which the work outlined in the working drawings is to be done and exactly what type and brand of wiring, plumbing, underfloor ducts, air-conditioning equipment, etc. are to be used. With proper working drawings and well-written specifications, the extent and character of the work that is to be done can be clearly understood by both the building owner and the contractor. These two sets of papers, then, serve both as a basis for bids from various contractors and also as a basis for agreement as to what the contractor selected shall do and what kind of materials he shall use in doing it.

Working drawings and specifications are the two most important supporting documents for the contract papers existing between owner and contractor. This emphasizes the need for ensuring their accuracy and completeness before competitive bids are sought from contractors, unless construction is to be handled on a cost-plus-fee arrangement. Drawings can be completed as certain construction work is put into motion.

WORKING DRAWINGS

Let's consider the typical drawings that must be made to form a complete set of working drawings for an office building project. In general, the set will include detailed drawings of the building, of the office layout for each floor, partition drawings, structural drawings, plans for electrical layout, underfloor-duct layout, plumbing, heating and air-conditioning systems, each supplemented by explanatory drawings showing representative sections of each layout in minute detail.

For an example of working drawings, let's look at some of the typical sheets that were used to make up the set for the functionally shaped office building of the Bird Company, shown in Illustration 19-1. The site plan is

Illus. 19-1. (Left) Rendering of building.
(Below) Photo of completed building.
(Bird & Sons, Boston Mass.)

shown in Illustration 19-2. While the construction drawings are shown in part plans at reduced scale, they will indicate the detail necessary to ensure that the contractor knows what is to be done in each step of his work.

Office Layout Drawings (Illustration 19-3). The location of private and general office areas, with names of departments and individuals, special areas, and all pieces of major office equipment, is shown on this full drawing. Telephone and other electric outlets are also shown. Office layout drawings are usually made by the architect and are the drawings which coordinate the physical, mechanical, and electric elements of the building and which are the basis of future expansion.

Architectural Partition Drawings (Illustration 19-4). Separate partition drawings are made by the architect. On these drawings location of partitions influenced by the electric, mechanical, and underfloor-duct systems is shown. The detail drawings indicate use of fixed metal, masonry, wood, and other types of partitions by means of various symbols and indicate whether the partition is to be permanent or movable, of the rail, dwarf, 7-foot, or ceiling-height type. They also indicate materials and treatments for exterior walls.

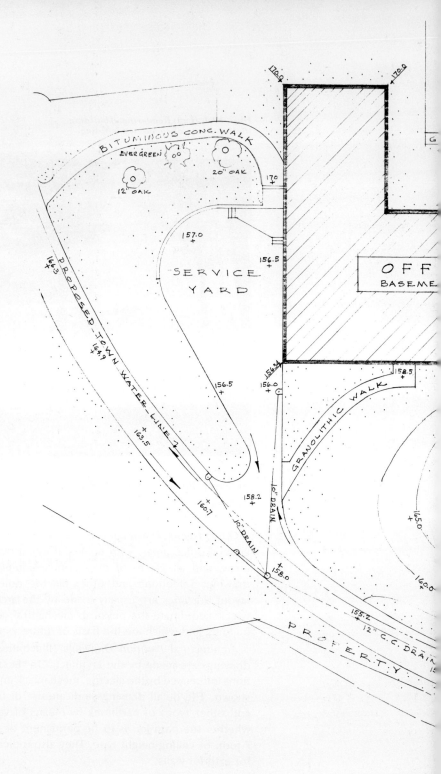

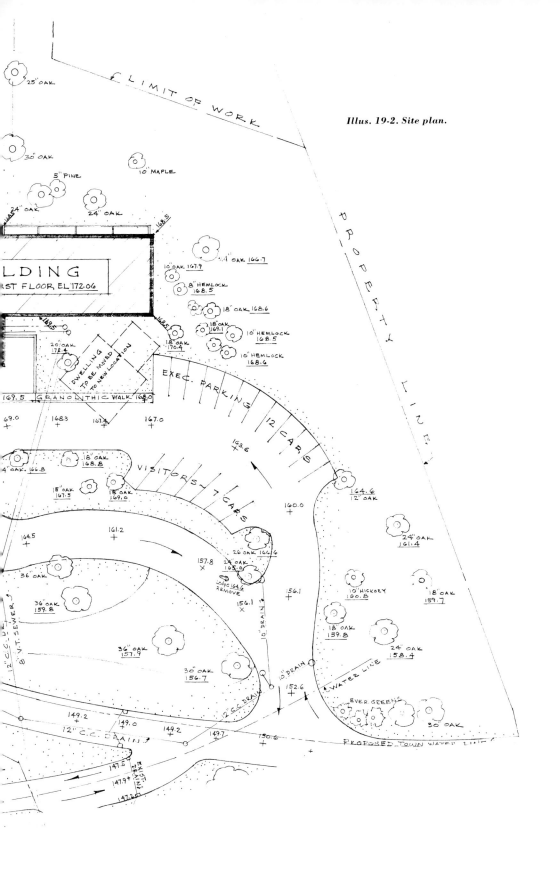

Illus. 19-2. Site plan.

Illus. 19-3. Office layout drawing (part plan). (a) First floor.

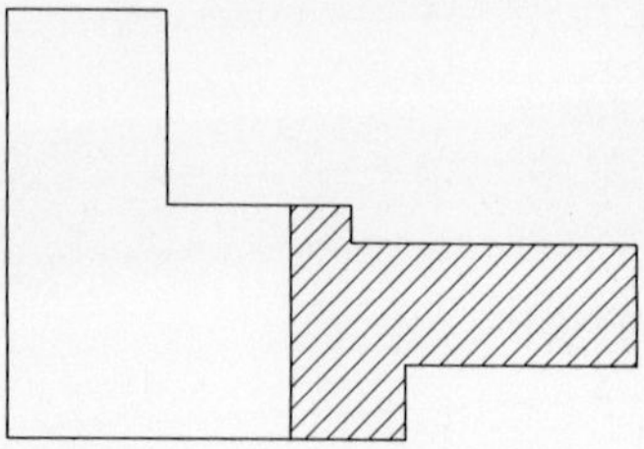

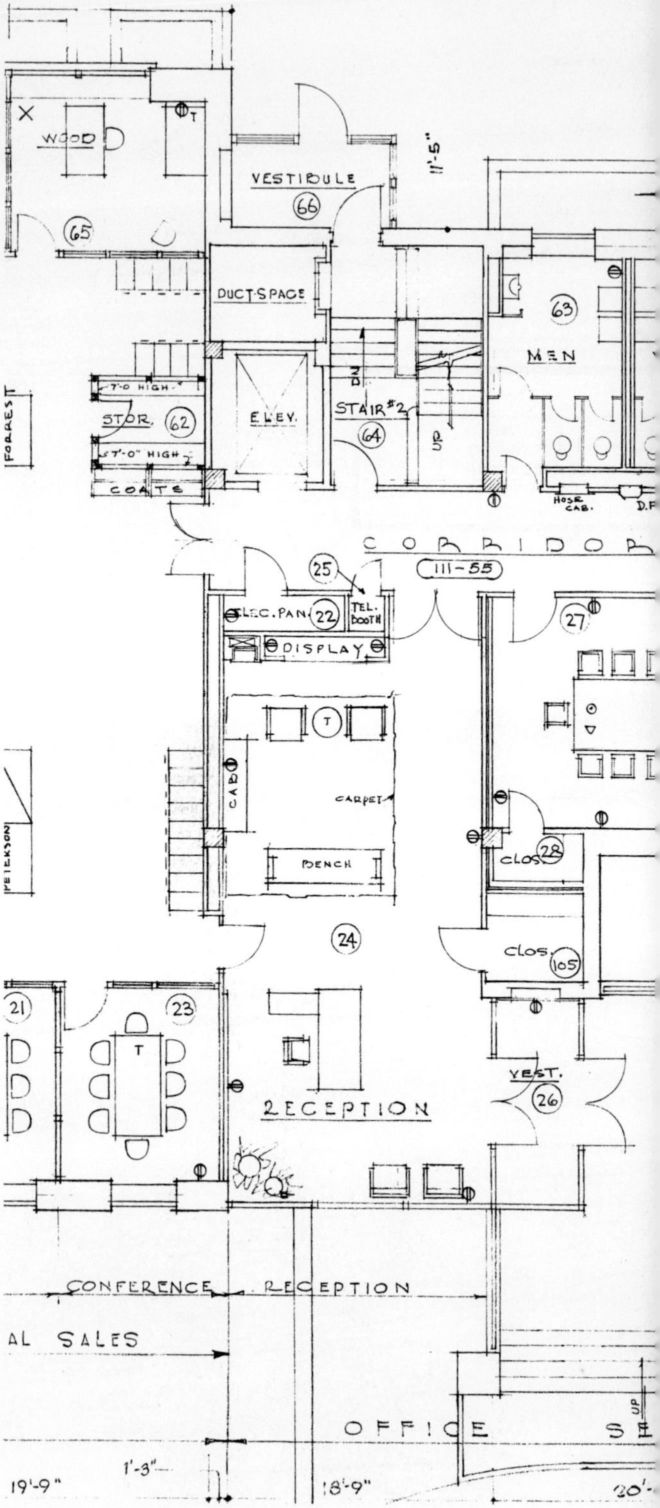

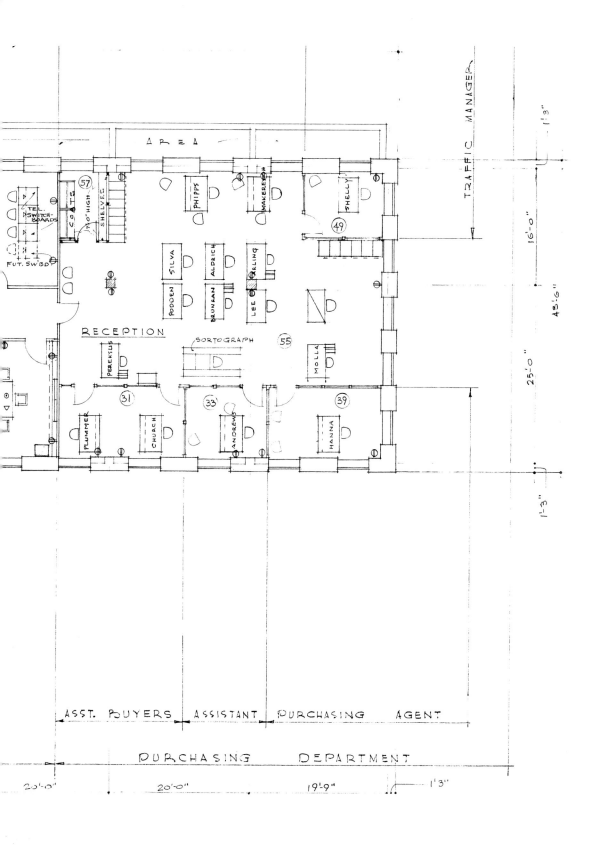

Illus. 19-3 (Cont.) Office layout drawing (part plan). (b) Second floor.

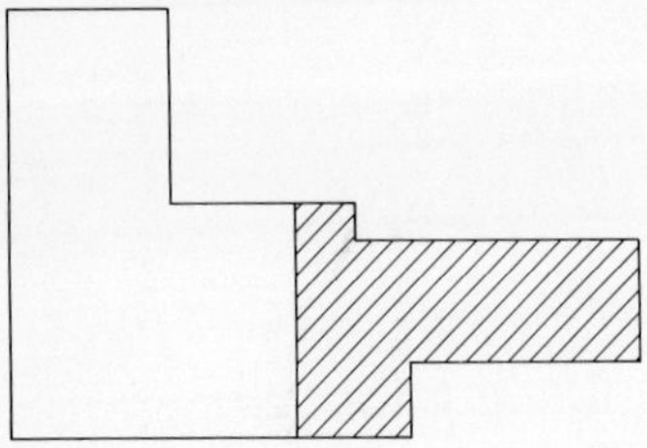

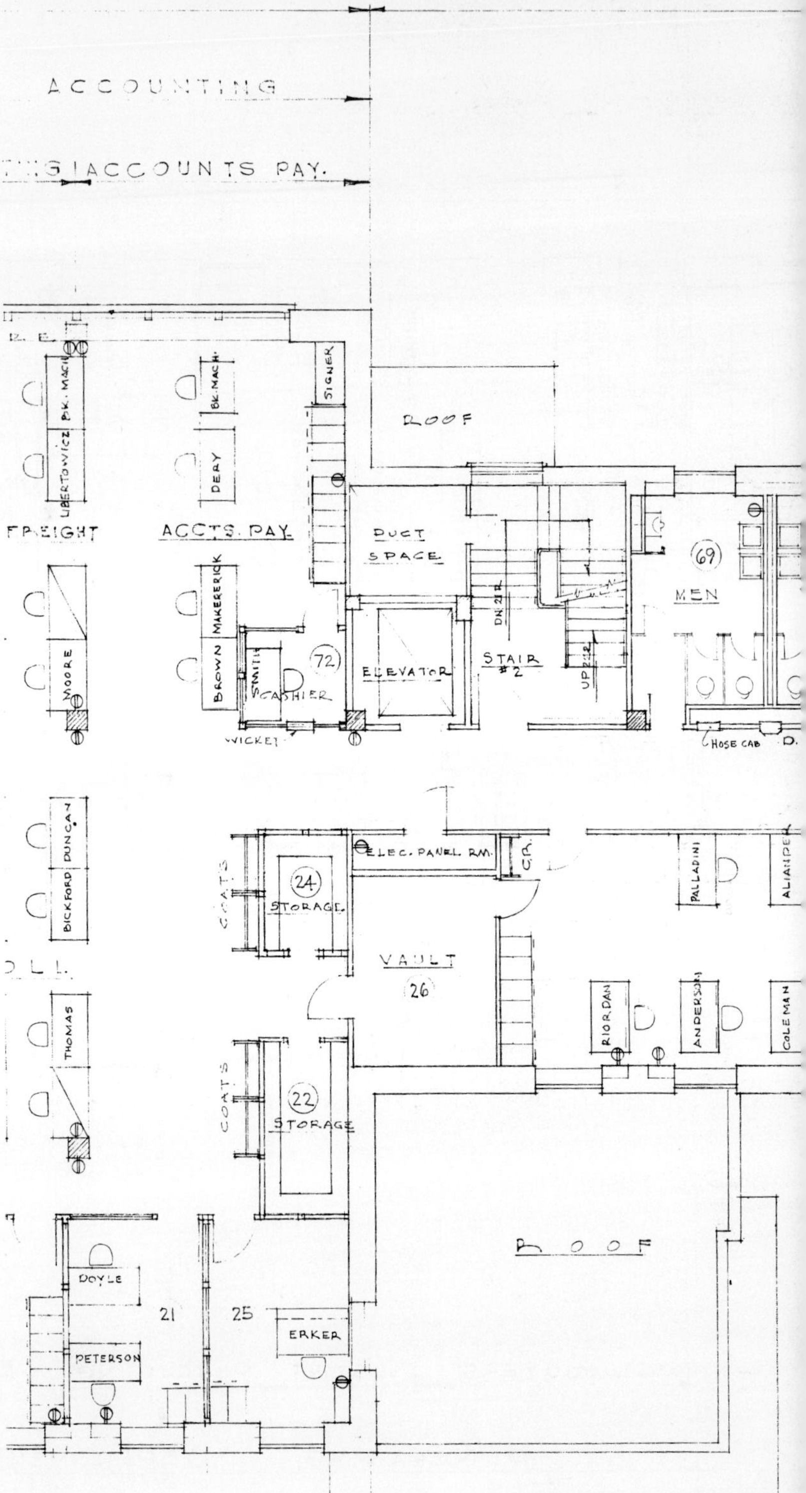

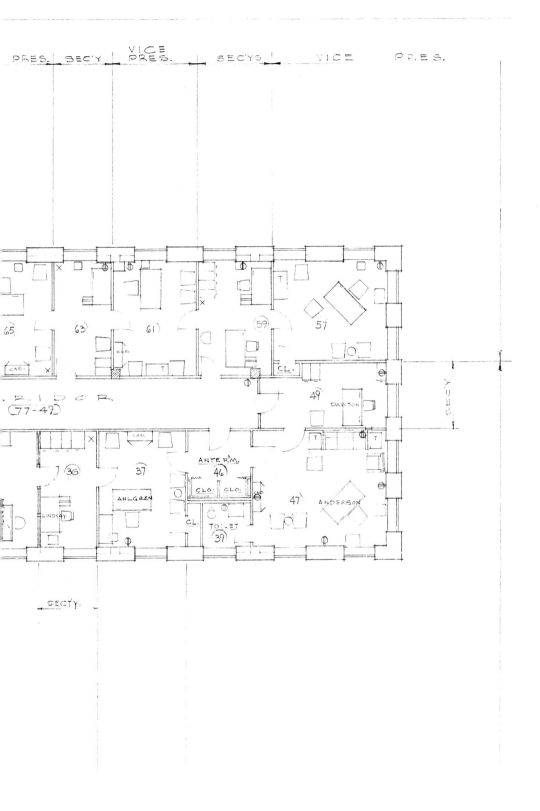

65 63 61 59 57

CORRIDOR
(77-49)

49 DAWSON

SECY

36 37 ANTER'M. 46 47 ANDERSON

AHLGREN CLO. CLO.

LINDSAY CL. TOILET 39

SECTY.

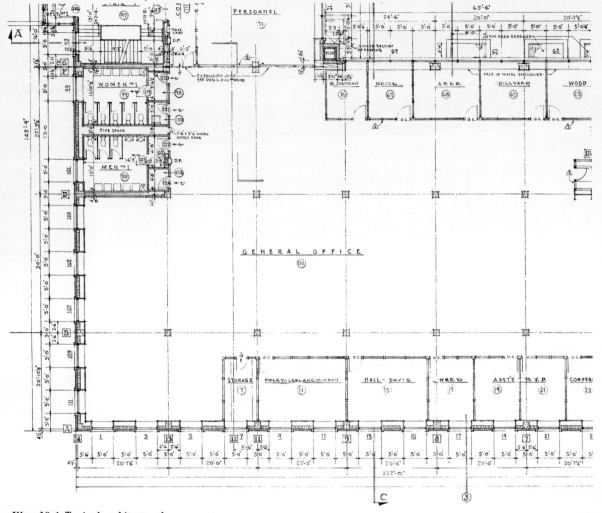

PERSONNEL
71

PERSONNEL

WOMEN NO 1
99

MEN NO 1
104

GENERAL OFFICE
111

B. JOHNSON
70

NEISE
67

ABER
68

HILLYARD
67

WOOD
65

STORAGE
7

FOLEY-LEBLANC-MURPHY
11

HALL-DAVIS
13

WEED
17

ASST'S TO V.P.
19

CONFER
23

Illus. 19-4. Typical architectural and partition plan.

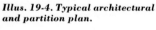

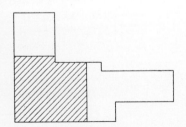

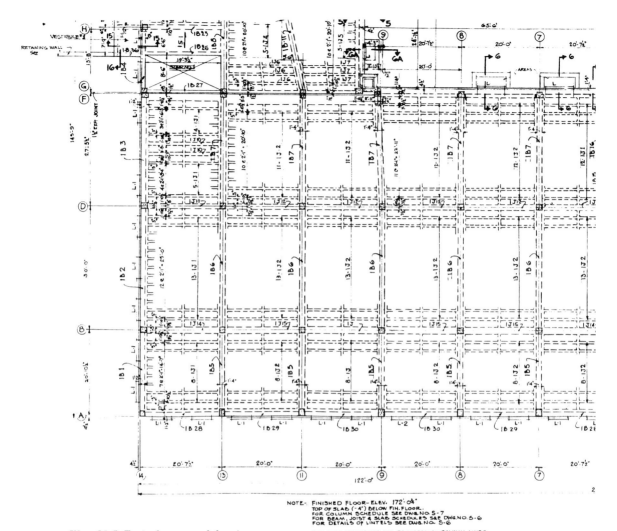

Illus. 19-5. Typical structural drawing.

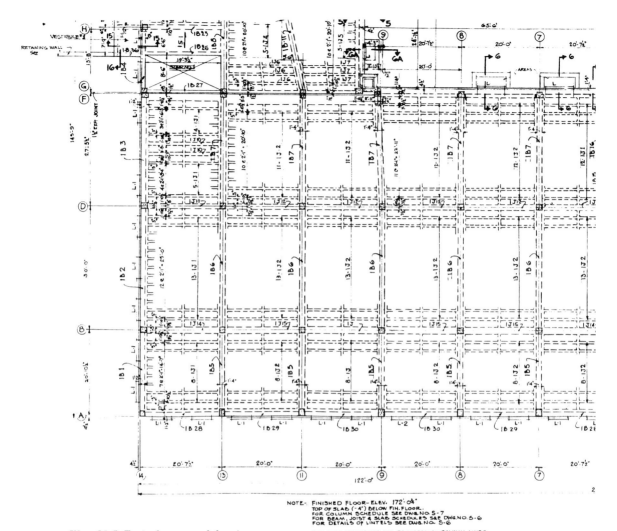

NOTE.- FINISHED FLOOR- ELEV. 172'-0".
TOP OF SLAB (-4") BELOW FIN. FLOOR.
FOR COLUMN SCHEDULE SEE DWG. NO. S-7
FOR BEAM, JOIST & SLAB SCHEDULES SEE DWG. NO. S-6
FOR DETAILS OF LINTELS SEE DWG. NO. S-6
COLUMNS AND BEAMS ARE CENTERED ON COLUMN LINES
UNLESS OTHERWISE NOTED.
BRIDGING JOISTS ARE IN CENTER OF BAYS EXCEPT WHERE OTHERWISE NOTED.

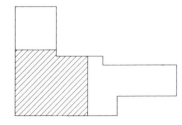

Structural Drawings (Illustration 19-5). These drawings show the construction of the building. They show in detail, besides exact dimensions of the building, how walls and windows are to be handled, location of all steel and concrete elements in the building, the method of enclosing steel columns, where air-conditioning units are to be located at windows, and the column-center dimensions. They also indicate the type and locations of interior walls and the general structural method to be used in constructing the building.

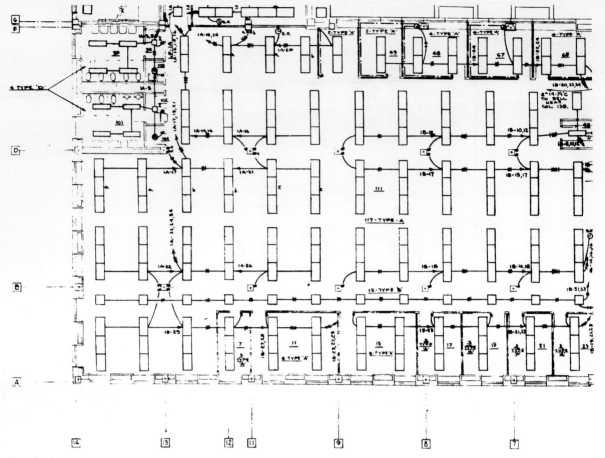

Illus. 19-6. Typical electrical drawing.

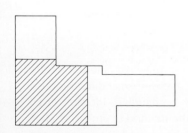

Electrical Drawings (Illustration 19-6). Another group of drawings included in a set of working drawings shows the electric elements that must be installed. The over-all lighting-fixture layout is indicated, and details of the drawings show the switch controls and circuiting of all individual fixtures and switch controls. The capacity of power lines necessary for each floor of the building is also shown, as well as the type and capacity of wiring necessary for individual areas.

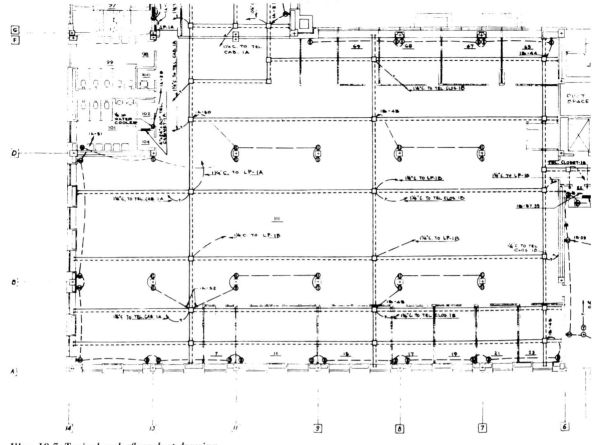

Illus. 19-7. Typical underfloor-duct drawing.

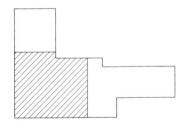

Underfloor-duct Drawings (Illustration 19-7). Sometimes, if the building under construction is not too large or complex, underfloor-duct drawings may be combined with either the structural or electrical drawings or both. In large or complicated jobs, however, separate drawings are required to show the over-all plan of the conduits that supply telephone and electric outlets throughout the office areas. Detailed plans indicate locations for pull boxes, junction boxes, insert locations at desks and machines, and similar information.

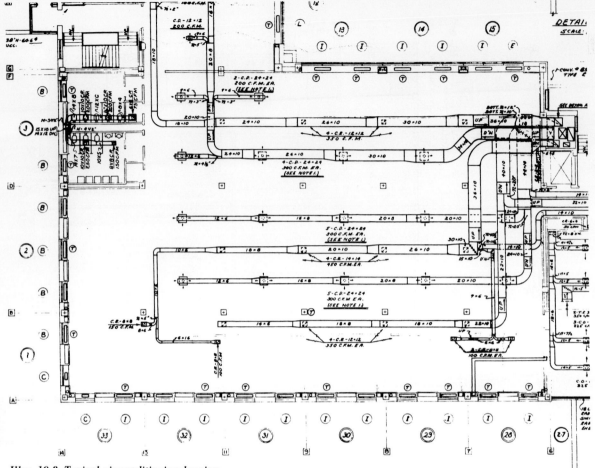

Illus. 19-8. Typical air-conditioning drawing.

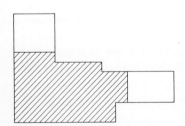

Heating and Air-conditioning Drawings (Illustration 19-8). These two systems may require separate drawings or may be combined in one plan. Again the amount and complexity of the work will determine whether these drawings must be made separately. In general, these drawings will show the supply and return pipe-lines for the heating system, the locations of valves, and the sizes of pipe to be used. The air-conditioning drawings show the distribution-and return-duct pattern from vertical and horizontal shafts to various locations in the office. They also show the location of cooling equipment, fans, and services. The detail drawings indicate how general office bays are conditioned and how private-office window units satisfy the functional modular arrangement of the buildings.

SPECIFICATIONS

When the working drawings are nearing completion and most of the decisions have been made, the specifications are written. The specifications for a building are divided into sections which correspond to chapters in a book. Each section covers the work which will probably be done under a single contract or subcontract. Usually each contract or subcontract will cover a single building trade, but practice varies in different parts of the country.

The arrangement of the sections of a specification usually follows the general schedule of dealing with the various trades on the actual construction job.

The title page of a specification gives the identity of the owner and the project and describes the contract documents. Following this, the invitation to submit proposals or notice to contractors may be included for convenience of reference. Neither of these documents, nor the instructions to bidders, is really a part of the specifications or of the contract papers, but they may be bound in with the specifications. The instructions to bidders usually give information as to the form of contract, method of payments under the contract, and the method of analysis and comparison of bids.

The general conditions of the contract and any special conditions for the general contractor come next in a set of specifications. After these follow the precise specifications for each of the various construction trades. A table of contents or index is useful but not always included.

It should be explained that the *General Conditions of the Contract* is a standard, detailed form available from the American Institute of Architects, The Octagon Building, Washington, D.C. Among the topics covered are extent; correlation and intent of documents; detail drawings and specifications; ownership of drawings and models; surveys, permits, and regulations; protection of work and property; inspection of work; supervision; changes in work; delays and extension of time; correction of work before and after final payment; applications for payments and certificates of payments; insurance; relations of contractor and subcontractor; architect's status; arbitration; cleanup.

CONTRACT DOCUMENTS

While the working drawings, the general conditions of the contract, and the specifications are the most important contract documents necessary to perform any architectural work, there are two other important agreements which will enter into the building or altering of any space. One important document is the owner-contractor agreement which is discussed in the next chapter. The other is the owner-architect agreement.

Owner-architect Agreement. This document covers the work to be performed by the architect and the method of payment for his services by the owner. In general, this agreement includes paragraphs covering the architect's services, fees, costs, payment, surveys, borings and tests, supervision of work, preliminary estimates, ownership of drawings, successors and assigns, and arbitration clauses.

There are many ways of paying an architect for his services. Listed below are the five most common methods:

Type	Provisions
Percentage of the cost of work	The architect receives a fee proportionate to the total cost of the structure. Extra fees for construction changes thus automatically adjust to cover extra time spent by the architect.
Fee plus cost	The architect is paid for all his costs including office overhead and drafting plus a fixed fee.
Lump sum	The architect is paid one agreed-upon amount which does not change regardless of changes in construction. This arrangement is most satisfactory on large projects.
Per diem rate	The architect is paid a certain per day rate for all work done by himself and his staff, regardless of how many days are involved.
Salary	Sometimes an architect is employed by an organization for the time required to do his work. He works in the company's quarters and is paid a fixed salary.

The percentage-of-the-cost-of-the-work and fee-plus-cost arrangements are the most common forms of agreement between architect and client. Lately we hear of the fee-plus-cost form on contract in combination with a maximum wherein owner and architect share the savings. Maximum costs are usually based upon scope specifications, sketch drawings, and contractor's budget estimates. Per diem and hourly rates are sometimes used in combination with these contracts for monthly billing and net costs of services and share in any savings with standard control terms as a guaranteed maximum fee.

twenty

ESTIMATES, CONTRACTS, SCHEDULES, AND CONSTRUCTION

With working drawings and specifications completed and with solicitation of estimates for the cost of construction and the final signing of agreement with the selected contractor over, one is prepared to go ahead with the construction of the building. But before we discuss construction, let's see how estimates are made. What indication does a company have of the approximate cost of a new building *before* calling for bids? What control does it have on costs?

BUDGET AND CONTRACT ESTIMATES

The executives of any corporation must know in advance how much it will cost to remodel space or build a new building. The amount of money to be spent is a company decision; the architect is usually informed during the preliminary study stage what the company consideres a target budget figure. This preliminary budget is usually regarded by the architect as a guide which, of course, may be revised upward or downward as the preliminary drawings are developed.

When the preliminary designs become reasonably fixed, the corporation may request an estimate of the cost of construction. The architect, on the basis of his preliminary drawings and an outline of specifications, can secure rough estimates to confirm his budgets. It should be understood, however, that the architect is not responsible for the accuracy of such early estimates as the general contractor is for his estimates when final working drawings and specifications have been completed.

Architects' estimates are made on the basis of their own knowledge of the field. Over the years every architect keeps abreast of unit costs of labor and materials. From this past experience, through the personal research of his office and by means of current construction-trade reports which he studies constantly, it is quite possible for an architect to establish a reasonably accurate budget for a project. Sometimes he figures costs on the actual basis of materials and labor, as a general contractor will eventually do, but more often he arrives at his estimated, rough total cost by computing costs per square foot or cubic foot of building space and then by multiplying this figure by the number of space units in the proposed building.

The architect's rough budgets are guides to the owner. Obviously they help the owner decide in the first place whether it is wise to build at all. Since they also outline the comparative costs for the alternate systems, techniques, and finishes that can be used in a high- or low-cost building, they also help him to decide how he is to build and what extra facilities or expansion space is to be included in the building.

One of the main purposes of the preliminary estimates is to get budget information firmly fixed so that the company can authorize the architect to go ahead, to prepare final working drawings and specifications based on the decisions that have been made as to how the proposed building will be constructed.

When the actual working drawings and specifications have been completed, several building contractors will analyze them and submit final bids to the owner. If requested, the contractors will give "bid bonds" with their bids, ensuring completion of the work for the owner if the bid is accepted.

OWNER-CONTRACTOR AGREEMENT

When an owner decides to accept the bid of a given contractor and is ready to start construction, he will want to execute an owner-contractor agreement. This contract will state the work to be done by the contractor and the method and amount of payment by the owner for his services. There are two basic types of agreement: one is a lump-sum contract, the other is a cost-plus-fee agreement.

Lump-sum or stipulated-sum contracts apply when the contractor names a definite figure for constructing the building. Obviously, such a bid must be based on a clear and definitive set of drawings and specifications. The contractor's bid figure will include his overhead and profit.

An owner's invitation to bid under such a contract usually includes the following information:

1. Location where proposals will be received
2. Date of delivery for proposals
3. Place where the contract documents may be examined or secured
4. Amount of deposit for securing copies of drawings and specifications
5. A brief description of the proposed building

Cost-plus-fee contracts are also commonly stipulated in soliciting bids for a new building. They provide the same end result as a lump-sum contract, but the contractor's estimate is broken down to show costs of the building and percentage or fee to cover the general contractor's overhead and profit. Although a budget may be agreed on, this arrangement does not guarantee a ceiling cost as the lump-sum contract does. It does offer two advantages, however: both owner and architect know the itemized costs of each subcontractor's work, and it is possible to let various subcontracts before all the working drawings and specifications have been completed.

Under the lump-sum agreement, obviously all working drawings and specifications must be completed down to the last detail before a contractor can estimate costs for construction as a basis for a bid. In fee-plus-cost arrangements, the owner, architect, and contractor jointly award all work to subcontractors by mutual consent. Since there is no absolute fixed figure to which the contractor is bound, work can start on the building before final drawings and specifications have been made for every detail of construction. The owner is protected against exorbitant and unexpected costs by the proviso that he and his architect must approve all subcontracts.

The flexibility provided by the cost-plus-fee contract can mean considerable savings of both time and money on a major construction job. It does, however, involve added work on the part of the architect during construction and so implies an increase in his fee.

Completion Dates and Construction Schedules. Since completion dates for the building are included in the contract documents, all construction schedules must be directed toward the agreed-on dates. The typical construction schedule shown in Illustration 20-1 indicates how the time periods are broken down. You'll note that all construction or building trades are covered on the schedule. One of the newer techniques for scheduling is the critical path method. Walter Kidde Constructors, Inc. uses this method to schedule construction and describes it thus: "In this system, all activities are assigned a position and a duration in a sequenced network that graphically illustrates the project from beginning to end. Activities with long durations and many dependent activities are identified and linked together to determine the 'Critical Path' through the network. If activities on the critical path are kept on schedule, costly complications and delays are minimized." Computer techniques are used not only to schedule construction but also to program architecture and engineering work and to schedule moves.

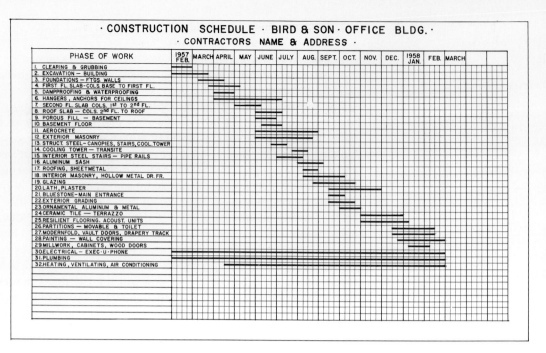

· CONSTRUCTION SCHEDULE · BIRD & SON · OFFICE BLDG. ·
· CONTRACTORS NAME & ADDRESS ·

PHASE OF WORK	1957 FEB.	MARCH	APRIL	MAY	JUNE	JULY	AUG.	SEPT.	OCT.	NOV.	DEC.	1958 JAN.	FEB.	MARCH
1. CLEARING & GRUBBING														
2. EXCAVATION — BUILDING														
3. FOUNDATIONS — FTGS. WALLS														
4. FIRST FL. SLAB-COLS. BASE TO FIRST FL.														
5. DAMPPROOFING & WATERPROOFING														
6. HANGERS, ANCHORS FOR CEILINGS														
7. SECOND FL. SLAB COLS. 1st TO 2nd FL.														
8. ROOF SLAB — COLS. 2nd FL. TO ROOF														
9. POROUS FILL — BASEMENT														
10. BASEMENT FLOOR														
11. AEROCRETE														
12. EXTERIOR MASONRY														
13. STRUCT. STEEL— CANOPIES, STAIRS, COOL. TOWER														
14. COOLING TOWER — TRANSITE														
15. INTERIOR STEEL STAIRS — PIPE RAILS														
16. ALUMINUM SASH														
17. ROOFING, SHEETMETAL														
18. INTERIOR MASONRY, HOLLOW METAL DR. FR.														
19. GLAZING														
20. LATH, PLASTER														
21. BLUESTONE-MAIN ENTRANCE														
22. EXTERIOR GRADING														
23. ORNAMENTAL ALUMINUM & METAL														
24. CERAMIC TILE — TERRAZZO														
25. RESILIENT FLOORING. ACOUST. UNITS														
26. PARTITIONS — MOVABLE & TOILET														
27. MODERNFOLD, VAULT DOORS, DRAPERY TRACK														
28. PAINTING — WALL COVERING														
29. MILLWORK, CABINETS, WOOD DOORS														
30. ELECTRICAL — EXEC·U·PHONE														
31. PLUMBING														
32. HEATING, VENTILATING, AIR CONDITIONING														

Illus. 20-1. Typical construction schedule form.

Progress Photographs. Owners, architects, and contractors like to have progress photographs made of their job as it moves from the first work on the site toward completion. Usually on a given date each month, three or four photographs, or as many as are necessary, are taken, showing the work that has been completed. Thus a pictorial record of progress is furnished the owner. These photos are used to support the contractor's monthly requisition for payment; the contractor includes progress photos with each requisition. Thus the owner can check the exact stage of completion of the building each month as well as the materials stored on the site, and can judge whether the requisition is justified by the work accomplished.

CERTIFICATES FOR PAYMENT

Certificates for payment are monthly requisitions to the owner to cover the amount of work completed by the general contractor and the subcontractor. These certificates, executed by the architect and supported by the contractor's bills, are sent to the owner for payment each month. The certificates for payment generally show:

1. Relationship of the amount requested to the total amount of the contract

2. The total sum requisitioned through previous certificates, the total payments already made, and the balance due, if any

A typical certificate for payment is shown in Illustration 20-3, which is accompanied by contractor's bill, Illustration 20-2.

| PROJECT: | OFFICE BUILDING
BIRD & SON
KENNETH H. RIPNEN CO., INC.
ARCHITECT | CONTRACTORS NAME
& ADDRESS | | |

ITEM NO.	DESCRIPTION OF ITEM	ORIGINAL OUT- SIDE CONTRACT PRICE	REVISED ESTIMATED COST	% COMP LETE	AMOUNT COMPLETE TO DATE	AMOUNT PREVIOUSLY COMPLETED	AMOUNT OF THIS REQUISITION

REQUISITION NO.   DATE

Illus. 20-2. Contractor's requisition form.

BUILDING DEPARTMENT PERMIT

Before construction begins, most communities require that building plans be approved by the local building department or building inspector. This is necessary to ensure that the building will conform to local structural safety and exit regulations and to ordinances covering plumbing and electrical work. If no local building codes apply, new buildings must conform to a state building and labor code.

SUPERVISION

It is standard practice to have the architect responsible for the plans supervise the construction of a new building or the alterations of an old building. The architect visits the site as often as seems necessary to make sure that work is moving forward at a satisfactory rate and that the owner's interests are being protected. This does not, however, imply daily superintendence of the work. On a large job, a resident architect (a representative from the architect's office) will be employed for these supervisory responsibilities, as well as a clerk-of-the-works whose job is mainly administration.

When the owner and the architect agree that the details of a project require additional or special supervision, an owner-architect's office is established at the site to ensure close supervision of all phases of construction until the building's completion. This is particularly important during electrical, plumbing, and air-conditioning work. When this is required, it is customary for the owner to reimburse the architect for these additional services.

Illus. 20-3. Certificate of payment and statement of account.

KENNETH H. RIPNEN COMPANY, Inc.

Date of Issuance...

No. of Certificate...   Job No.............................

CERTIFICATE OF PAYMENT AND STATEMENT OF ACCOUNT

This is to Certify that, in accordance with the terms

of a contract executed the..day of..195......

by and between...Contractor

and...Owner for

....

There will be due and payable from the Owner to the Contractor, upon the...................day of............................

the sum of..

....$...............

Comments...

The status of account under the above contract is as follows:

Original contract sum ....$...............

Additions to date: ....

....

....

....

Original sum plus additions ....

Deductions to date hereof ....

Contract sum at date hereof ....Total

Total certified, to date ....

....

....

....

....

Amount of this Certificate ....

Leaving not yet certified...

KENNETH H. RIPNEN COMPANY, Inc.

....

....

The Contractor, having examined the above statement of account, finds it correct and acknowledges receipt,

upon the.., 19..........., of the amount above certified.

....Contractor

FORM 126 1M 4-58 H&S

WINTER CONSTRUCTION

In the past it has been customary to delay work on large projects during winter months in the Northern states. Architects and builders today, however, strongly endorse a start-to-finish building program without breaks, even though it may mean construction through the winter.

The reasons for continuing construction through the winter are all financial. Perhaps foremost among the reasons for a continuous building program is the fact that once a corporation has authorized a new building, it needs it as quickly as possible. It usually does not plan a new office building until its current quarters have become overcrowded and outmoded, conditions which in turn make for lowered efficiency in its offices. Thus in terms of the company's own internal operating conditions, the faster it gets its new office building, the sooner it can achieve top operating efficiency.

And, even aside from this factor, other savings possible through continuous construction more than compensate for the 1 or 2 per cent increase in contractor's costs that may be expected if work must be done through the winter.

The cost savings possible through continuous construction are many. It is possible to order materials at the most favorable market rate. Continuous labor-wage increases in the construction trades often mean a rise in labor costs if there is a two- or three-month delay in the building program. Continuous ordering of materials also guards against possible shortages which could develop if construction work were halted. And finally, a continuous building program makes it possible to order all building materials on a continuous-flow basis, thus doing away with the need for large material storage areas at the site.

As an example, an architectural firm, in starting a typical large two-story office building in the Albany, New York, area, was able to recoup for the client the extra construction costs involved in building through the winter by finishing the costly masonry exteriors of the building before a spring wage rise and increase in costs of materials went into effect. And, of course, since the company was able to occupy its building several months earlier than would have been possible if work had been stopped during the winter, it also gained savings in its own operating costs.

Again, in this particular case, a halt in construction until spring would have meant that many building facilities could not be installed in time for fall occupancy. Thus, if winter construction had been ruled out by the owner and architect, there would have been a second winter holdover before completion of the building. As it was, the company was able to move its staff into the new offices in the fall of the following year, fifteen months after construction had begun.

It is the architect's responsibility, if he sees that winter construction will be necessary, to ensure that contractors with winter building experience

are chosen for the job. There are certain definite techniques that have been developed that make winter construction perfectly feasible, even though unit costs will be slightly higher than they are during spring, summer, and fall. Huge protective tarpaulins, about 200 by 30 feet in size, are draped over the scaffolding allowing workers easy access to the sides of the building from bottom to top. Both scaffolding and covering are moved wherever they are needed as construction progresses. Salamanders (a gas heating device) are used inside the sheltered area created by the tarpaulins to keep temperatures well above freezing. This is a necessity not only for the workers but for the protection of the building as well, since fresh masonry is badly damaged if subjected to freezing or subfreezing temperatures before it has hardened. Newly developed antifreeze materials and special quick-hardening cements, however, can be used to speed the drying process and to ensure that the masonry will not be damaged by winter temperatures.

Winter construction is stressed, not because it is desirable in itself, but because it is more desirable than halting work from fall until spring. The constant upward curve in the over-all costs of building will almost always mean that total construction costs will go up if work is halted for several months. Moreover, in the very states where winter construction may pose the greatest problems in terms of protection of workers and the building, it eases another problem—labor availability. Thus, the Northern states are a very reliable construction-labor market during the winter months because the pace of construction does fall off then. Bricklayers, for instance, normally in short supply during the spring, summer, and fall, are easily available to any contractor with a winter building schedule.

Still, wherever possible, building construction should be scheduled so that exterior work at least will be finished before severe weather begins. Normally, architectural plans and drawings should be made during the winter months, so that construction can start first thing in the spring. The architect will always counsel his corporation client to start work in the spring, if it can be done, so that the building can be closed in by fall. Interior work can then be carried out through the winter without any difficulties or special protective arrangements.

Unfortunately, such ideal scheduling is not always possible, and so we must resort to winter construction.

twenty-one

THE OFFICE OF THE FUTURE

We have analyzed the methods by which a new office can be made truly new, can be made to embody the most modern principles of space planning and administration, can be made a functional mechanism, contributing—through its structure and physical channeling of the work flow—increased efficiency to the office and the personnel who work in the office.

We have described how the future needs of the office, as well as its current needs, can be met by providing expansion space both within an existing building and through preplanned additions to the existing building, so that the office constructed today can still prove adequate to company needs for fifty years or more after its construction. We have discussed the ultimate office building in terms of its structure and design.

But what of the ultimate future of the office? What will be the typical office of the next century? City or country? Skyscraper or horizontal building? A centralized or decentralized organization?

We think the pattern of tomorrow's office is already foreshadowed by the "offices" that have been established by a few leading companies today. It will be a very different office from the clerical complex we are accustomed to today. It will be an office in which the twin developments of instantaneous world-wide communications and practically instantaneous electronic processing of clerical data will be the determining factors. It will be an office which can take on the major share of routine, clerical data processing for a large national company and yet perform equally efficiently in a suburban area or in the heart of a major city.

For instantaneous communications have offered the office which functions mainly on internal clerical tasks as much mobility in location as the modern office has achieved in interior space planning. A private wire-communications network can be centered anywhere, country or city, and the electronic data-processing equipment which functions as the heart of that network works equally well in the center of Manhattan or hundreds of miles from a major city.

The first major communications center of this sort was established by Sylvania Electric Products, Inc., in a little town called Camillus, near Syracuse, New York, in 1954. Why Camillus for a company which had always had its headquarters in New York City? Camillus was chosen because of its pleasant suburban location in the Syracuse area; the Syracuse area itself was specified because it was shown by linear programming that Syracuse represents the approximate geographical center of the greatest flow of Sylvania message traffic.

In other words, location depended not on commercial services or transportation facilities but on the message load on private wire services. The place in the nation which was most central in terms of the flow of data from Sylvania transmission points was the best place to establish the new office, or rather the new data-processing center.

For this is the other face of the coin as far as the "office" of the future is concerned. Centralized electronic data processing means a drawing back of clerical facilities from plants, sales offices, and regional administrative offices across the country to one central point. But it does not necessarily mean that the processing center at that point will be the office as we know it today.

For the "center" of the data-processing center will be the electronic equipment which will digest the great mass of information flowing in from all parts of the country and turn it into the reports, the analyses, the forecasts of trends that management needs to guide the business. The same computer will prepare the payrolls, the social security reports, the great number of individual papers needed within the company for its own internal operations. The great number of clerical workers needed in offices operating today with manual processing methods will not be needed, although technicians and clerical workers trained by the company to a high degree of specialization will be.

And it is precisely this center which can be located anywhere in the country the company wishes or finds desirable.

Thus, when we predict that the office of the future will be a centralized office which has assumed the great majority of all routine clerical functions for all company operations, it does not necessarily mean that that same office will also function as the national administrative center. For the same miracle of practically instantaneous communications which makes the clerical data-processing center possible also makes it possible to divorce routine, clerical data processing from the administrative headquarters of the company.

Again we see how electronics and communications make the utmost mobility possible for the office. All the operating information management needs to run a company can be transmitted in summary from the data-processing center; decisions based on that information are made in the home office.

Thus mobility in the office of the future will be carried to the point where functions which formerly could be separated by only a floor or two within one building, where executive offices were located on the top floor and general offices on the floor below, can now be carried out in entirely different locations.

All these factors will serve to make the office of the future an entirely different entity from the office of today. We have seen offices in the past traditionally placed in one of two locations: at the major plant site or in a major city. In recent years, there has been a trend to the suburbs, but the suburbs chosen were usually suburbs of the city where the offices had formerly been located. In effect, they represented location in a remote area of the city.

Now with divorce possible between the administrative decision-making headquarters and the processing and reporting headquarters, it becomes possible for the processing functions to be located almost anywhere even though, in most cases, the administrative headquarters will probably locate in the most convenient urban and suburban locations for some time to come.

The sociological effects of this change will probably be profound, for this means that the majority of office workers in any one company can be moved away from a city location without the company's suffering any disadvantages through loss of personal contact at the top echelon with the concentrated commercial facilities of the city.

Although, as has been pointed out, an electronic center can be located anywhere, the probability is that the great majority of companies will locate their centers in suburban areas near the city which houses the administrative center, or alternatively, at one of their major plant sites.

But this will have a profound effect on the city as we know it today, since it will mean dispersion of a large number of the city's workers into surrounding suburban areas, a much wider dispersion than anything we have seen to date. And it will in turn mean that services and facilities needed by those workers will be drawn away from the city with them. New social, recreational, and health facilities will have to be set up for the employees. Housing will have to be provided for them. Shops will have to be established to meet their daily needs. So additional people to staff all these facilities will be pulled from the central city into the surrounding suburban areas.

All this will probably eventually lead to fundamental changes in the circumscribed, highly concentrated city that we know today, in which a comparatively small central area holds most of the working population during the daytime, and to the rise of the metropolitan area as the basic urban unit. There the central city would continue to exist as a general administrative, financial, information, and cultural center, but a large part of the population would be dispersed through a very wide surrounding belt where their homes would be near their work, a situation not possible today when people may live in the suburbs but must go to the city to work. The whole complex would represent a new type of social and civic organization, a blend of suburban and urban qualities unlike anything we know today in either city or suburb.

This relocation, even though it occurs over a long period of time, will bring on a change, or perhaps an acceleration, in social trends. Inevitably, companies will become more paternalistic to employees as these employees are relocated. When any company sets up a location in a new area, it must assume new responsibilities toward its employees; it must aid them in finding living quarters, must help them with moving expenses, must, perhaps, set up transportation facilities for them.

As the trend toward creating mass clerical data-processing facilities in new locations continues, we can expect to see all these patterns become more pronounced, for as more and more companies move some of their facilities to new locations, it will become more important than ever for them to induce their workers to move with them. The large labor market will remain in the central city through the first phases of the transition, and office workers will be at a premium in the suburban districts. Thus companies may very well have to give substantial financial aid to employees wishing to build homes in the new locations and will have to make some provisions, either independently or in cooperation with local suburban authorities, for strengthening recreational, educational, medical, and other civic facilities in the area selected.

This new and increasing paternalism will be reflected within the offices and factories of the company, too. Recreational areas of all types will continue to grow more numerous and more elaborate. Medical care, provided by the company not only for employees but for their families, will become more common. Artificial sunlight for workers in both offices and factories will become a standard, as will the introduction of germ-killing agents in the conditioned air circulating through the working areas.

And, as the inevitable trend toward consolidation of more and more companies into giant concerns continues, some of the largest will undoubtedly reach the point where it occurs to them that, with 5,000 to 10,000 office workers, they have the nucleus of their own city, that it is not really necessary for them to locate in proximity to any major center, that they can establish a sizable community of their own anywhere in the country they wish—Wisconsin, Rhode Island, Florida, or Arizona.

For the office with 5,000 to 10,000 or more employees will become more and more common in the future. And 5,000 to 10,000 workers concentrated in one place represent a potential community, when families and necessary civic and commercial services are added, of 50,000 to 60,000 people—a respectable city.

Why should a company set up its own community?

Part paternalism, part self-interest. The ultimate step in providing for the employee is to provide for all his needs, to establish the community in which he lives, and to provide all its services. And from the company viewpoint, there are positive gains to be realized. A company can locate its headquarters in a low-income area and then, still at less cost than it would face in competing for labor in a high-salary market, offer better than the prevailing wage rates and living conditions more attractive than the standard for the region. It not only will attract high-caliber people—once it has attracted them, it will keep them.

Thus, ultimately, we can expect to see a revival of the "company town," although it will be a far cry from the grim and dreary factory towns of the past. For this company community will be located in the spot that is ideal for living conditions, not ideal in terms of its proximity to coal pit or iron fields. And people will not be held in the company town of the future by low wages and poor education which bar them from moving or finding other jobs. Rather they will be attached because the company enclave offers better living conditions and security than they can find elsewhere.

And so the larger corporation can benefit in terms of survival, of holding its own working force, not just for the working life of each individual but for generations, by establishing its own self-contained community.

All these things can be foreseen as a result of the changes in the office made possible by better communications techniques and the development of electronic data processing. The social, economic, and political effects of the transition will be profound, and they will be mixed. Some effects will be good, some bad.

We said at the beginning of this book that the office, as it grew larger and its responsibilities grew more complex, faced the problem of taking measures designed to prevent its workers from becoming automatons. We said that the great challenge facing the office was keeping things in human scale, preserving each worker's sense of individuality, through provision of the proper physical and personal environment. But, however good the environment created within an office, the increasing difficulties of commuting to work in the city, of traffic in the city, of the overpowering concentration of workers in a few square miles every day from nine to five will defeat everything any given office can do to maintain the human scale, unless the pattern of dispersion predicted here should come about.

We have established in the past a pattern in which company working centers were massed together in one gigantic urban business district, forcing workers for the entire area to establish their homes around the central district. As the central business district grows, the perimeter of homes and apartments becomes an ever widening ring until the point is reached where workers are traveling hours each day to get from home to work and back again.

We must reverse that pattern, breaking off pieces of the central business complex and reestablishing them as relatively isolated centers of employment where workers can live in close proximity to their work. This will also relieve pressure in the central city; it will in effect spread a net of relatively small neighborhoods, incorporating both homes and business areas, over a wide region in which there is less congestion and less pressure at the core, more facilities and working opportunities at the perimeter.

City and country will represent different aspects of one community rather than entirely separate entities as they do at present.

The architecture will be understandable in that in some areas the outward appearance of buildings will be dictated by the conservative, traditional neighborhood, community, or part of the country in which it is to be built. In some cases, the façades and building mass will probably be in one of the colonial, French, English, or Spanish styles or their modifications.

Other neighborhoods will permit a purely functional type of structure. Such contemporary architecture will permit the outward appearance of the building to express the functional elements of the organization and building's use. All the elements of structures and communities will be brought together in a dignified harmonious mass, which is really the contemporary architecture for today and tomorrow.

And in the long run this will be healthy, in terms of the people who create our business fabric and who are the reason for its existence, for it will mean that each person has a much freer choice of how he wants to live and work than has ever been possible in the past. Those who like the open, quiet semirural life will be able to find careers in the new centers of employment which are devoted to one company and which have as their hub that company's data-processing center with its attached buildings housing the company's administrative and middle-echelon groups. Those who want the good life within a paternalistic company atmosphere, which will give them employment when they get out of school and which will see them through their retirement years as well, will also find the values they seek in such centers.

And for those who enjoy the faster-paced life of the city, the stimulus of constant contact with people outside the company, the chance to forge ahead through more challenging jobs in a flexible labor market where high turnover creates more opportunity, the city will still be there. But it will be a city in which relaxation and living space will be easier to come by than they are in today's crowded metropolis. It will be a city in which the worker can, just like his colleague in the suburban area, live within reasonable distance of his work and live in pleasant and spacious quarters.

And so the social changes that will result from the double impact of instant communication and electronic processing of paper work, no matter how many problems they bring, will eventually benefit the nation in terms of the ability of each individual to find the type of work environment and the type of social environment that best satisfy him.

The office of the future will offer employees a much wider range of desired qualities, through its locale, its attitude toward its employees, its existence as the center of a "company community" in suburban or developed metropolitan areas, than can today's office. And somewhere within this range, each worker can find the "human scale" that most closely meets his needs and ambitions.

In this respect, the modern office building is unique because no other structure—pyramid, cathedral, hospital, home, school, or factory—has ever been quite like it. In a way it is a symbol of the ultimate achievement of a machine age—a building which serves as administrative and planning center for a machine society—and a building in which machines themselves are relatively insignificant.

For that is the most important fact about modern office buildings: They are the largest and most complex structures ever built solely for human beings and to answer human needs.

The human factor must be predominant in offices. Factories are built around the machines they house; an office building is, or should be, built around people and the functions it houses. But office functions are carried forward primarily by people rather than by machines. Moreover, an office does not ordinarily find it possible to employ the straight-line work flow characteristic of a factory, and its needs and requirements vary more than do those of the factory.

Thus an office must be planned so that its departments, though broken down into separate units, still function as a cohesive whole. It must also be planned so that its space is flexible, so that the size and grouping of these units can be changed rapidly to meet varying needs.

As a result, an office building, perhaps more than any other type of structure, must be planned as a dynamic building, one adaptable to interior change. An office may have as few as 10 people, or as many as 10,000. Its equipment may be simple, or it may run the gamut all the way up to giant computers—which require a large amount of space—special electric wiring, sound conditioning, and elaborate air-conditioning equipment. Thus, designing living and working space for office workers according to the best principles of modern architectural engineering and designing techniques represents a challenge to architects unlike any other they may face.

Compare for a moment the requirements of an office building with those of practically any other modern structure. Our houses, schools, hospitals, civic, institutional, religious, and other buildings, once they have been planned and built, are more or less static in floor layout plan. Their interior layout is permanent. Their exterior structure by the same token is usually fixed; if expansion is required at some time in the future, a separate new building is constructed. The office building, by contrast, must allow for extreme fluidity within its walls and, more and more often today, must also be built so that future additions as preplanned expansion can be made to the building itself.

This new concept of the office as a fluid and expanding organization, requiring working space that is also fluid and allows for physical expansion, is a development mainly of the last forty years. In that period the clerical and administrative load of American business has expanded enormously. Thus architects and engineers who specialize in the office field and assist clients in continued office space administration have had to develop entirely new techniques to meet the growing complexity of the office's requirements.

We have seen the advancements that have taken place in office building design and engineering. The buildings of the twenties were designed to depend on natural ventilation and, to a large degree, on natural light. That is why space was not very deep and the window provided light and air. Even such buildings as the Empire State and the Rockefeller Center complex represent a concept of the office building as a shallow structure with rental space constructed around a center service core containing elevators, stairways, utilities, and toilet facilities, as stated heretofore. Such structures give offices maximum possible exposure to exterior light and air and are built primarily to satisfy rental of divided floors. But with the great improvements in artificial lighting and the development of year-round air conditioning entirely different building concepts have become practicable. Note the newer buildings of Rockefeller Center and the larger office centers of the country. It is now possible to build deep space in buildings, with interior working space uninterrupted by service facilities—which can also be located off to one side—and still make office space in such buildings efficient, functional, comfortable, and healthful.

With the expansion of the office function, however, and the possibility of large, open interior space to house office workers, a new problem presents itself in the space-planning function. Management, in creating its organization structure, systems, and staffing, and the architect and engineer, in designing the physical facilities for the organization, have had to bear in mind that office workers, far more than industrial workers, must have a sense of identity with their organization and an over-all understanding of all its functions, along with better facilities, if they are to do the best possible work. Neither management nor designer can afford to forget that the office worker is a human being and that every component part of his environment must not only stress human qualities but also better enable him to realize his part in the organization as a whole and his contribution to that organization. Thus, as the size of offices has increased, it has become increasingly important to design offices in such a way that the individual worker does not become submerged in a great mass of fellow workers. The office worker's environment must be kept in human scale if we are to have the best and most efficient clerical procedures and orderliness and cleanliness are the bywords today.

Now that the problems of supplying large, uncluttered, open working areas are being overcome structurally and mechanically, everyone responsible for the administration of office space will be concentrating on the new problems of giving large office buildings this human scale in which the worker will continue to function as an individual rather than a cog. The human being—not the machine—is the most important unit in the office.

These are the major factors creating the new science of office-space planning and administration: the new dimensions of the office; the new possibilities for open, unbroken space in the office created by mechanical advances in lighting, air conditioning, sound control, and construction techniques; and the need to handle large groups of people and large areas of space in such a way that each worker can do the best possible work in the best possible pattern. Within this framework, a whole variety of proven techniques has been developed to achieve the best possible utilization of space in terms of the company occupying that space and of the morale and productiveness of the company's workers. These techniques have been outlined in terms of interior-space planning, office furniture, standards for control, and total integrated environmental modularity for a company's office space. It is the responsibility of an office space administrator within the company to use these techniques to provide a proper working environment with him receiving the full support of top management.

INDEX